I AM
SPEAKING

ALSO BY BEVERLY BARTLETT

The Lord's Garden
God Still Speaks, Are You Listening?

I AM
SPEAKING

Beverly H. Bartlett

Orchidia Publishing
Cleveland, Georgia

ISBN-13: 978-1-7349398-0-4

Printed in the United States of America.
9 8 7 6 5 4 3 2 1
First Edition: February 2020

Cover Design by Matt Smartt

TABLE OF CONTENTS

I AM
SPEAKING

TO MY CHURCHES

A Living Sacrifice

God's Church is a living Body
Not a dead form.
It is a place of humility and suffering
Not a stage on which to perform.

Too many times we serve men
And do things to boost our own ego.
The honor all belongs to God
For we are simply told to go.

Our own position and prestige
Amounts to nothing in God's eyes.
We build on our own agenda
And this thinking, God will despise.

Our prayers are often lacking
Until our hearts cry out in earnest.
We must bear each other's burdens
Especially for those in the refining furnace.

The more we pamper our flesh
The more attention it will need.
We are to deny ourselves, take up our cross
Be slow to move, let Jesus lead.

We must offer our lives each day
They should be a living sacrifice.
Then our joy will be overflowing
And God's promises will suffice.

Anorexia & Bulimia

We have spiritual anorexia and bulimia
In our churches today.
These are detrimental to the body
And there is a price to pay.

Anorexia is spiritual starvation
It makes one unsteady, unsure, and weak.
They don't know God's word to stand on
Then they are easy to defeat.

Those with spiritual bulimia
They eat large spiritual meals.
Then they vomit them all out
So, wisdom is not revealed.

There is no productivity in their lives
No obedience, no discipline, no application.
Their lives are empty of meaning
And nothing brings them gratification.

We must council them before it's too late
Return them to a healthy regime.
Then they will walk in wholeness
And regain their self-esteem.

BREAD

Christianity is one beggar telling another beggar
Where he can find bread.
Many people feed their physical body
But few are spiritually fed.

Just as life without food will perish
So, our spiritual life withers away.
We may not even notice
Until we wake up one day.

We wonder what is happening
Our joy in life has disappeared.
We are anxious and discouraged
We're afraid, as before we never feared.

Return to your first love
He is waiting anxiously for you.
We can't face this life alone
Without Jesus we can't make it through.

He is our Bread of Life
We partake of Him each day to survive.
Then as we start flourishing spiritually
All our senses come alive.

Life is filled with new meaning
We face trials unafraid.
To live our lives for Jesus
Is the smartest decision we ever made.

CLONES

Each individual is different
God made us to be unique.
You may resemble someone else,
But there is always that little tweak.

God does not make clones
Not even in a snowflake.
We are much more important
And God doesn't make a mistake.

Each Church should be different
Not a copy of another one.
God is not interested in numbers
He just wants His work to be done.

Just ten people sold out to Jesus
They do more than one hundred lukewarm.
Those who don't know spiritual warfare
Do not help, but only cause harm.

They stop the flow of the Spirit
Who always shows us the Way.
As we listen and follow Him
We'll move forward without delay.

Let's embrace our differences
Refuse to be a clone.
God will be pleased with us
As we leave our comfort zone.

FOR MATURE BELIEVERS

BE STILL

Be still and know that I am God
My grace is freely given.
I don't need more work, Bible Study, or prayer
I never intended you to be driven.

It's not by works, but by My Spirit
That you please Me the most.
It may be just quiet time spent with Me
When it's works you tend to boast.

You constantly think you have fallen short
When you don't pray or study enough.
But in the scheme of eternity
All this is simple stuff.

You don't have to do it all
Just enjoy the things I have made.
Now you're really living
You're my child, no longer a slave.

If I want you to perform some task
I will speak and let you know.
If I want to send you somewhere
I will equip you and expect you to go.

Quit striving to try to please Me
Be content just being My child.
When you learn to relax and enjoy My company
That's what makes Me smile.

GLUE

Holy Spirit, You are the glue
That keeps us from going to pieces.
Without You to lead and guide us
Our ability to cope nearly ceases.

When we ask and someone says "I'm fine"
They're probably insecure, neurotic, and emotional.
They don't want to murmur and complain
For they are just trying to be sociable.

We are to share each other's burdens
For we in Christ are one.
We celebrate when one is honored
And weep when they are undone.

As we function in God's design
Our church will be healthy and complete.
A beautiful field for the harvest
There aren't any tares, just wheat.

GOD'S GRACE

We say grace before our meals
Gracious in hosting friends.
Grateful for someone's kindness
The list goes on without end.

The church proclaims the "Gospel of grace"
Does the world see it when they look at us?
Do we welcome the prostitute and the poor
Or do we turn away in disgust?

Jesus associated with the dregs of humanity
He touched a leper who was unclean.
Do we dare minister and care for those with AIDS?
Or consider them unworthy to redeem?

God's grace and our grace
Seem like two entirely different things.
His stems from a heart of love
While ours to reason clings.

We believe a good theology of grace
But that's not the way we live.
Do we understand God's unconditional grace
And His readiness to forgive?

God gives grace to the undeserving
And we all fit in this category.
When we learn to extend His grace to others
We will see more of God's glory.

HIDDEN

When you look at our human body
Most of the organs are hidden inside.
But we can't get along without them
Not even if we tried.

No one but God can see our heart,
But without it we would die.
We don't understand how it keeps on beating,
Yet this truth we can't deny.

Our brain is a giant computer
That keeps everything in order.
Our muscles and ligaments hold us together,
Much like bricks and mortar.

So it is with Christ's body, the Church
Most of the workers are out of sight.
Without each one's cooperation
It would be harder to win this fight.

When we all work together as one,
Our Church will be like a magnet.
The Holy Spirit will draw them in
We won't have to use a dragnet.

Our Community will begin to change
For our love will be clearly seen.
God will be exalted
And He will reign supreme.

His Grace

There's a place of peace in Jesus
That's not found on the outside.
It's that inner feeling
Where we rest and then abide.

It's like a pasture beside still waters
Where our soul finds its nest.
Away from the turmoil of the world
A place of perfect rest.

Here we find restoration
From the trials and cares of life.
There is quiet and stillness all around
No sign of anger or strife.

We can go there as often as we like
For Jesus has prepared this place.
He is always there to meet with us
Another facet of His grace.

TO MY CHURCHES

In Step

Stay in step with Me
Don't run ahead or lag behind.
Only in close proximity
Can you sense what's on My mind?

I know the plans I have for you
They will bring honor to My name.
To reach those others have forgotten
Don't worry about wealth or fame.

These things are of the world
Their pleasure is only temporary.
But the future they produce
Is really very scary.

The narrow road is difficult
Self-control is required.
But the character that it builds
Will always be admired.

The fellowship in church we share
As each obstacle is left behind.
Excitement around each corner
That will boggle the mind

You've left the masses on the broad road
As you keep in step with Me.
New horizons loom before you
For your spirit's been set free.

To soar to new heights
To see what I have in store.
As you accomplish each assignment
I'll show you even more.

Your reward is My companionship
How precious our walk together.
My peace and joy will fill your being
And this, no enemy can sever.

JESUS EXAMPLE

Jesus, You came to earth in human form
And You taught us how to live.
But most important of all
You taught us how to forgive.

There are so many people out there
With un-forgiveness in their heart.
So many have been hurt by others
Their lives have been torn apart.

Yet You forgave those who crucified You
Can we do anything less?
If someone has not been born again
They may be doing their best.

We can't look in a person's heart
Nor see the motive for their action.
That's when the trouble starts
We show the wrong reaction.

When we are motivated by love
We will see both sides of the issue.
Then we can bring about reconciliation
And not let this cause a fissure.

Jesus came to set the example
Now it's up to us to continue the work.
To set an example of love and forgiveness
Even if the person is a jerk.

We all fall short of perfection
So, don't be the one to judge.
This world will be a better place
When we refuse to hold a grudge.

LITTLE – MUCH

Little is much when placed in the Father's hand.
This saying is oh so true.
When we willingly give of what we have
He is wisdom – we don't have a clue.

Remember the five loaves and two fish.
They were enough for the hungry crowd.
So, when we offer what little we have
We are humble in His sight – not proud.

We usually feel inadequate
We see such need everywhere.
But God will put us in place
And we are to minister there.

We may think, "What good can we possibly do?"
Just offer it and trust Him with the outcome.
Then, we are in for a surprise
For it's always enough – and then some.

God always blesses our offerings
No matter how meager they seem.
He will use them to build His Kingdom
And many souls He will redeem.

So, let's always be quick to offer what we have
Then sit back and watch in surprise.
It's always amazing what God can do
With what seems so small in our eyes.

My Love

My love for you is so deep
That you will never understand.
I knew you before you were born
Your name is engraved on the palm of My hand.

I will never leave you nor forsake you
No matter how far you stray.
My Holy Spirit will continue to draw you
And show you a better way.

To live a life that is meaningful
That will shed light along the way.
There will be trials and tribulations,
But I will guide you through each day.

I desire that you spend time with Me
Putting all other things aside.
I'm preparing you and grooming you
To be My beautiful bride.

A Church that brings Me honor and glory
For all in the world to see.
One that has triumphed over evil,
Because you belong to Me.

PLAYING CHURCH

Time is too short to be playing Church
We need to be about the Father's business.
Only as we win souls and make disciples
Will our efforts be a success.

Our Churches are falling short of the goal
When they are just keeping people comfortable.
We don't want to offend anyone
This is a bunch of bull.

Jesus did just the opposite
He ridiculed this form of religion.
Maybe we need to get people riled up
So, others' opinions don't matter a smidgen.

We need to see weeping at the altar
People brought to radical transformation.
This next generation is headed for ruin
For lack of Kingdom revelation.

We need to wake from our stupor
Satan is winning this battle.
Let's rise up with prayer and action
Then the gates of hell will rattle.

Refuse to be intimidated
God is always by our side.
When He sees that we are sincere
We'll begin to turn this evil tide.

PRIORITIES

Where on your list of priorities
Have you put prayer?
When it is at the bottom
Then you wonder why I'm not there.

You put preaching, praise, programs,
And projects in first place.
Then add prayer as an afterthought
You forget to seek My face.

I am not pleased with My Churches
When they neglect this important part.
You've mixed up your priorities
When you put the horse behind the cart.

What happened to all night prayer meetings?
Or fasting and prayer for your breakthrough?
These were prevalent in previous revivals
And this practice still stands true.

If you want your church to prosper and grow
Seek My face first of all.
Then I will move mountains to bless you
And I'll listen when you call.

RENT

Think of the tithe as the rent we pay
For this space on earth we occupy.
Compared to most accommodations
A tenth is really not that high.

The fresh air that we breathe
The rain and the sunshine are all free.
Even the lightning that clears the air
God has provided for you and me.

We only give when it's above the tithe
And giving brings our souls delight.
Selfishness darkens the soul
Giving opens the door to light.

We may not be led to serve overseas
But we can send or support someone there.
This brings us much satisfaction
When we know we've done our share.

Alms are added to the tithe and giving
When we go out of our way to help the poor.
We'll find we can never out give God
As we give, we receive even more.

We are here to be good stewards
Of all God puts in our control.
As we fulfill our duties faithfully
It brings more pleasure than silver and gold.

Revival

When Pastors and Christians get hungry enough for You
And fall on their knees and pray.
Then You will hear from Heaven
And hear what they have to say.

If it's Your will and their hearts are pure
Then revival will surely come.
It will sweep in like a hurricane
It will be totally awesome.

Signs and wonders will take place
Healing and deliverance as well.
Like a tsunami it will flood the area
And conquer the forces of hell.

God will show Himself to be mighty
Impacting all places around.
The results will be souls for His Kingdom
Freedom for those who were bound.

Then we wonder why we waited so long
To pray as a body for revival.
When the world gets darker and darker
This will ensure our very survival.

Now we praise God for what He's done
What only the Holy Spirit could do.
To think that this momentous event
Was just waiting on me and you.

SAFETY

We are only safe from the ravages of life
Under the shadow of God's wings.
Floods, hurricanes, and tornados
And the destruction of these things.

Diseases that were once eradicated
Are brought in by refugees from other lands.
New and weird bacteria and viruses
But we're safe in the protection of Your hands.

So, we pray like never before
That men will turn from their wicked ways.
Realize they are lost without Jesus.
That riches and pleasure are a passing phase.

We will all face Your judgment one day
And it will be just and fair.
We'll cuddle up close in Your presence
Safe from this present nightmare.

SHAKING

The end times are getting closer
God's shaking has begun.
He will start with His Church
She will be number one.

Pastors who are out of order
They will be pushed aside.
New ones will be installed
To prepare His beautiful bride.

Some partners will suddenly leave
The ones who are unequally yoked.
In the end times we must be strong
The fires of passion steadily stoked.

If your partner leaves
Don't think you are to blame.
God has moved them out of the way
So, they don't extinguish your flame.

Churches may be split apart
Many will be closed and forgotten.
They weren't preaching the Word
Their foundation was rotten.

So be prepared for change
It is God taking action.
Guard your heart and mind
From any distraction.

We must learn to stand strong together
While all this is taking place.
Soon we will win the victory
And see Jesus face to face.

SINNERS INTO SAINTS

Church is meant for sinners.
So, God can change them into saints.
He changes us on the inside.
Removes that disgrace that taints.

Everyone wants to be needed.
To feel like they belong somewhere.
As we make room for those others cast out.
They will know that we really care.

It doesn't matter what you look like on the outside.
With your tattoos, or outlandish dress.
As long as you have a heart for Jesus.
He wants you to have His very best.

Just as too much inbreeding makes us weak.
Diversity will make us strong.
There is a place for your gifts and talents.
So, come on in where you belong.

THE BRIDE

Jesus isn't coming back for a trashy bride
One just like the world she is in.
She must be holy and spotless
For His Blood washed away her sin.

The Church looks so much like the world
You can't tell them apart.
She is seen as a hypocrite
This must break the Father's heart.

Will we repent and turn from our sin?
Prepare ourselves for our Groom.
Time is growing short
He will be returning soon.

Will our Church be the foolish Bride
The one who is left behind?
When Jesus comes looking around
His beautiful bride to find?

We'd best get our act together
Clean up the spots, wrinkles, and blemishes.
So, we will be ready when our Bridegroom comes
And not found left on earth's premises.

THE CROSS

It's only at the cross that our sins are forgiven
Only at the cross we find strength to go on.
When we see the sin running rampant
Our self-confidence is gone.

Jesus is our only hope
Neither government nor riches will suffice.
Men will stumble and fall
Our rock will always be Jesus Christ.

We cling to Him and His mercy
Something we don't earn or deserve.
He came to earth as our example
Of how we must love and serve.

No matter the rejection we face
We must stand firm to the end.
God has called and equipped us
To block this downward trend.

Security as we know it will dwindle
Lies and intimidations will take their place.
We must shine even brighter
So others will enter the race.

A race to the foot of the cross
Where we willingly lay our lives down.
There may be loss on this earth
But in heaven we'll receive a crown.

THE GOOD SHEPHERD

Jesus is both the Lamb of God and
The Good Shepherd
Two entirely different roles.
As the Lamb He died on Calvary
As ransom for our souls.

As the Shepherd He leads and guides us
Through life which is a maze.
But when we follow faithfully
His peace and joy will fill our days.

On the other hand, we see the goats
Who are stubborn and want their own way.
They are constantly getting into trouble
And refuse to submit and obey.

The Shepherd still cares for them
He goes out to find the lost.
He brings them back in His arms
To the fold – safe from the frost.

His patience is beyond our understanding
He counts the sheep He knows His own.
Some still refuse to stay with the flock
They prefer to go on alone.

It breaks the heart of the Shepherd.
To lose even one of His sheep.
But if they just continue to stray
The price they pay will be steep.

THE HEAVENLY VISION

The only way God places His saints
Is through the whirlwind of His storms.
They come in many shapes and sizes
In different and dangerous forms.

Are you living in the light of your vision
Or are you an empty pod?
Are you relying on yourself
Or have you put your trust in God?

We can't decide where we will be planted
Or we will be weak and unproductive.
We may think we are doing God's will,
But it will always be destructive.

Be content until God sends you out
Don't move until He does it.
Seeds will be scattered all over the place
And many souls delivered from the pit.

Always be faithful to your Heavenly Vision
Wait for it – though it tarries.
It will be worth the waiting
When you see the impact it carries.

THE MITE

What I can give may be a widow's mite
But God can multiply what I give.
When we all put our gifts together
They may enable someone to live.

There are so many needs around us
It's hard to know which to choose.
But if I ask, God will show me
So my gift won't be abused.

Sometimes greed gets in the way
And very little gets to the needy.
But God sees the motives of everyone
And He knows the ones who are greedy.

So, I never feel that my gift is too small
Even pennies add up you see.
As I give with a cheerful heart
Then Jesus will be pleased with me.

THE PAST

Once we put our hand to the plow
We are told not to look back.
When we keep reliving the past
It's revealing a deep lack

Of trust in the Lord
Who has taken care of our past.
We must move forward in today
To bear fruit that will last.

This reveals our doubts
In our Father's ability.
The future looms before us
He knows what He wants us to be.

Workers in His vineyard
Ministering to those in our sphere.
Revealing to them the word of truth
That will draw them ever near.

Where at the Cross of Calvary
Our past is buried, and God's love revealed.
We've been bought with a price
And our future is sealed.

We'll reign with Christ forever
What a wonder to look forward to.
Just keep your eyes on Jesus
And leave the past behind you.

THIS PLACE

What happens in this place
Needs to affect other places we go.
We come here to hear God's word
Now we have new seeds to sow.

We learn about forgiveness
How to care for the homeless and poor.
Now we have a greater incentive
To do more than we did before.

This is the place to come
To recover from your biggest regret.
A place where you can start anew
New patterns of thinking are set.

Give up your entitlement
Step down off your throne.
You'll find in this place
New interest you'll be shown.

It's time to stop running from God
And to meet Him face to face.
Now God will clean you up
For He is found in this place.

Maybe you've messed things up big time.
But God has plenty of grace.
You'll find people here who can help you
For there is lots of love in this place.

You'll learn how to connect faith to Christ
In your everyday life.
You'll discover the way of peace and joy.
It will replace anger and strife.

You'll find you're never more like Jesus
Than when you start to serve.
New avenues will begin to open.
That you feel you don't deserve.

TO MY CHURCHES

Now God has opened the artery
So we can begin to flow.
All over this community
Watch and see how this Church will grow.

TO FLY OR SIT

It's better to try to fly and fail
Than to sit comfortably in our nest and die.
The excitement and thrill awaiting
As we circle in the sky.

We were designed for heavenly places
Not this humdrum place below.
But the enemy wants to keep us grounded
He doesn't want us to know.

The thrill of soaring above our problems
Not being weighted down with sin.
When Jesus gives us freedom
Our flight can now begin.

Our circle of influence is small at first
But it will grow and expand.
The more time we spend alone with Jesus
The better we will understand

How to minister and pray in situations
For we know our flight plan.
Our controller is ever watchful
And success lies in His hand.

TRADITIONAL CHURCHES

Lord, there are so many of your Churches
That are still bound up in tradition.
It's like the members are prisoners
Locked up in detention.

They need to be set free
To know the joy of praise.
To be free to dance and shout
Or just their hands to raise.

Their pastors must be released first
For they hold the key.
Show us how to pray Lord,
To set these captives free.

Even in their worship and praise
They are performance driven.
Their love and care for each other
Is already given.

They haven't experienced the freedom
To become child-like again.
To worship and praise with abandon
Jesus, their Savior and friend.

WISDOM

I asked God a question about His word.
Why is wisdom called a she?
Most things in the Bible are about men
And they are called a he.

It's really very simple He answered
With the understanding it brings.
"Wisdom is a she
For Wisdom births many things.

She births people into ministry
Sometimes labor is involved.
She births much creativity
So many problems can be solved.

She births new ideas and gives insight
So My glory can be revealed.
I'm so glad I asked the question
Now in my understanding it is sealed.

Her riches are above rubies
How do we find this treasure?
God said to simply ask,
And He'll give to us with pleasure.

We must be God's children
To receive what He has to give.
Fear of God is the beginning of wisdom
And this is the life we should live.

I AM
SPEAKING

TO MY CHURCHES

PRAYER

ANGELS & DEMONS

Our prayers empower God's angels
What an amazing thought.
Why then are we so hesitant
To stop and pray as we aught?

When we forget to pray
The demons have the upper hand.
Someone who is hurting
Won't have the strength to stand.

We know that God depends on us
To pray and stand in the gap.
Or are we so callous and uncaring
That we really don't give a rap?

Prayer is more important than we realize
It can change a life and so much more.
If we understood what a difference it can make
We would pray like never before.

BACKBONE

The backbone of every church
Will always be its prayer team.
They are usually seasoned warriors
They recognize evil, seen and unseen.

The casual and Sunday-only Christian
Only wants to be entertained.
They are not interested in prayer
There is nothing there to be gained.

This core group will usually be small
But they are dedicated deep inside.
They know how to touch the heart of God
And the enemy is terrified.

When they are joined in unity
And all agree in prayer
The powers of hell are shaken
Many loosed from the devil's snare.

This role is of utmost importance
Without them the Church will be lost.
God is pleased when we pray
And the outcome will be worth the cost.

Be Careful

God forgives and forgets
Few people in Church have obtained this grace.
So many of our prayers should be specific
Not scattered all over the place.

Life is not always fair
But God is always faithful.
He is with us no matter where we go
For this we should be grateful.

When we pray according to Scripture
We know our prayers are heard.
The answer may tarry
But we stand firm in God's word.

Lives will be changed when we pray
So be careful what you ask.
We may need to disciple someone
Or maybe just pray and fast.

God makes the final decision
We just commit to do our part.
Our prayers are sweet incense to God
And He loves our tender heart.

Corporate Prayer

This is the most important weapon given the church
And yet one we seldom use.
That is why My Church is weak and frail
And My children are the ones who lose.

No wonder the enemy is wreaking havoc
Tearing families apart, shutting churches down.
Pastors giving up in despair
Satan has My children bound.

Prayer is the direct line to My throne
And I'm waiting anxiously to hear from you.
If you'll study My Word, you'll understand
That prayer brings strength, to make it through.

Corporate prayer is so powerful
It will destroy the enemy's stronghold.
When you all agree in My name
The world will stop to behold.

Power like they have never seen before
It will be like a nuclear bomb.
Whole cities will be affected
Then afterward, things will be calm.

People will be ready to listen
As My word is preached with power.
I'm waiting for My pastors to wake up
For this will be earth's finest hour.

FREE CHAPEL PRAYER GROUP

Just as a small rudder
Controls the ship's direction,
This small prayer group
Brings your church My protection.

A prayerless church will go nowhere
No matter the eloquence of its pastor.
They may hang in there for a while
But they are headed for disaster.

Don't grow weary or discouraged
I am here in a powerful way.
Numbers don't matter in My eyes
Even if it's only a few who pray.

When your hearts are totally Mine
And you put matters in My hand,
I will work miracles in your midst
And I'll give you strength to stand,

Against the attacks of the enemy
Who will try to discourage you.
But I will open your eyes
To see a totally different view.

Just as Elisha's servant's eyes were opened
You'll see chariots of fire all around.
The host of heaven is praying with you
For My favor you have found.

GRAVECLOTHES

Father, shake them out of their pulpit
For they really don't have a clue
What it's like to sit at Jesus' feet
To release control to You.

They know all about Jesus
But don't know Him as Lord of all.
Thousands sit in their pews each Sunday
Are they all headed for a fall?

They preach a message with their lips
But deny the power thereof.
They think those delusional who speak in tongues
And look down on them and scoff.

Lord, Satan has them blinded
Please open their eyes to see
That only as they make Jesus Lord
Will they and their congregations be set free.

Those of us who are Spirit-filled
Will continue to intercede.
To pray that their eyes be opened to the truth
So all of Your children can be freed.

OUR LACK – YOUR SUPPLY

Without signs, wonders, and miracles
Revival will not take place.
What is wrong in your Church, Lord?
Of power, there is not a trace.

The power that raised Jesus from the dead
Now resides in each of us.
We have failed in our mission.
Have we forfeited your trust?

Show us Lord, what is wrong
Something is blocking the flow.
This world needs revival
So, your power we must show.

Is it lack of prayer and fasting?
We've failed in both of these.
People are dying all around
From war and disease.

Holy Spirit, You're our teacher.
Show us how to pray with power.
To restore and save our brothers
Whom the enemy wants to devour.

Greater is He who is in us
So, we know that we can win.
We will see the victory.
Now give us boldness to begin.

Jesus, Jesus, Jesus.
You are all we need.
With Your power within us
We know we will succeed.

Rekindle The Fire

Lord, rekindle the fire inside me
Let me burn with passion for You.
I refuse to grow old and stale
I look forward to something new.

You surprise me all the time
Wondering what is next on your agenda.
I know that You can use me
All I need do – is surrender.

May the sparks from my enthusiasm
Set others around ablaze.
Then the world will look on in wonder –
They don't understand Your ways.

Now revival is on the horizon
It will sweep like a blazing flame.
People will fall down in repentance
And call on Your Holy Name.

You will respond to Your children with love
Welcome them into the family.
We've made an impact on this world
On this we can all agree.

Sold Out

I'd rather have ten people sold out to Me
Than a thousand who are lukewarm.
Prayer is just another duty
They think they have to perform.

I look on people's hearts
And I see the motive behind their action
They pick and choose like they're at the movie
And this is just another attraction.

Prayer is precious to Me
It touches the strings of My Heart.
That's how I see each one of you
You are special, I've set you apart.

To see what is on My agenda
And the things that I need in prayer
I know that I can depend on you
And you will always be there.

There is a special reward waiting
For those who put prayer first.
You'll find favor with Me and men
And your enemy, he is cursed.

Look To The Cross

We must look through the cross to see Jesus
Otherwise He is hidden from our eyes.
In the last days many will claim to be Him
But they are false prophets in disguise.

Even the elect may be led astray
By the signs and miracles they manifest.
So, pray for wisdom and discernment
Then we will stand firm in every test.

Learn and meditate much on the Word
So we won't be the ones deceived.
Be in intimate communion with Jesus
Then false manifestation won't be believed.

Cling to the Cross, for there is safety
In its shadow. We can stand strong.
The Holy Spirit is here to help us
To the Three-in-One we still belong.

THE SHALLOW THINGS

It's the shallow things in life
That keep us anchored to the shore.
It is in everyday living
That God can build and restore.

Then when we reach a pinnacle
We'll stand and not sway.
For God prepared us beforehand
And He will show us the way.

In the mundane things of life
We'll learn strength and courage too.
Then when we are far from shore
We will know how to make it through.

The storms and gales that come in life
Try to trip us and bring us down.
But we'll rise above the waves
With God's help, we will not drown.

God ordains the shallow things in life
To refine out the spiritual pride.
Never attain to be high and haughty
In simple trust, let God be our guide.

WATCH & PRAY

Since we took God out of the equation
Our Country has gone to rack and ruin.
We cast aside all morality
And lost our ability to discern

The difference between right and wrong
Each person going his own way.
God's Word says this leads to destruction
And we will face His judgment one day.

We as Christians sit back complacently
Watching this apostasy take place.
We need to rise up in indignation
And kick the devil out of this race.

Lukewarm is an abomination to God
Who has filled us with His power.
He expects us to use it
In this earth's final hour.

Judgment begins in God's house
His shepherds are the first to be shaken.
When we see this taking place
From our stupor, we need to awaken.

God is not a God to be mocked
He will cleanse those He called mine.
He will now separate the sheep from the sheep
Some to be saved, some left behind.

We are supposed to be watching and praying
Longing for Jesus' return once more.
He will come like a thief in the night
His kingdom on earth to restore.

I AM
SPEAKING

TO MY PASTORS

APPRECIATION

A BANQUET

Just as a Chef prepares his ingredients
I am preparing your congregation.
To you, being the Shepherd
I will give new revelation.

I will prepare the menu
Just go forth when I say move.
There will be obstacles ahead
But I will make them smooth.

The enemy has fought you long and hard
For he knows the difference you will make.
Don't let the opposition slow you down
This banquet is a piece of cake.

You will change the whole community
Then reach others far and wide.
Just continue to feed them My Word
I'm preparing a beautiful Bride.

I've gifted you in many ways
This banquet to prepare.
I will be the Guest of Honor
For My glory I will not share.

I will reward you in Heaven and on earth
For I know that you have done your best.
Continue to feed them tasty meals
And I will take care of the rest.

A Heart Of Love

I've given you a heart for My people
No matter their color or creed.
You have an encouraging word
To minister to each and every need.

I am training you now
For I have great things ahead.
As I am feeding you
Then others will be fed.

My words to you are life
A very precious seed.
You are sowing now a harvest
With your every special deed.

Do not grow weary and faint
At the varied and many tasks.
The harvest that you reap
Will be one that will last.

I see your tender heart
One that beats with My love.
Your reward will be great
When you reach Heaven above.

A PASTOR'S HEART

You have a true pastor's heart
Something that is rare.
Yours is not put on
For you really do care.

For My people who are lost and hurting
Caught in the enemy's net.
Unsaved, unloved, broken marriages
Distressed, floundering, or deeply in debt.

Just preach the words I give to you
For it's My voice that you hear.
Just stay humble and teachable
Never give in to fear.

You've a sharp mind and great intelligence
Listen close to the words I speak.
I will use what I have given to you
As it's always My will that you seek.

Each of My shepherds is unique
For the sheep in your pasture aren't the same.
So, your messages will each be different
For the honor must be to My name.

I have plans for your Church on the hill
That will draw people like a beacon light.
Disciple and train your congregation
So they will know how to fight.

The enemy will not give up easily
But with prayer and discipline stand.
I'm always beside you My son
For I hold your future in My hand.

APPRECIATION

We really appreciate all the things
That you speak and do.
God gave you a vision
And you always follow through.

Your family pays a high price as well
For you are pulled in so many directions.
But God sees every need you have
And He has promised you His protection.

You are teaching us many new things
To help us grow and mature.
Then it's up to us to listen and obey
So our salvation will be sure.

You have chosen a wonderful staff
To support and fulfill your vision.
You work well together as a team
With no strife, jealousy, or division.

As we embark on this new building together
May God orchestrate our every step.
Then may we as your congregation
Determine that each promise will be kept.

We know being a pastor is not easy
But it was God who did the calling.
You may not receive recognition on earth
But in Heaven will be the rewarding.

ASSOCIATE PASTOR

You are always behind the scenes
But I see all that you do.
You help with all the planning
And then you see it through.

I know your humble heart
And your sincere desire to serve.
One day you'll reap the harvest
And receive all that you deserve.

Keep My face ever before you
Turning neither to left nor right.
I'll always be there to guide you
And put your enemies to flight.

Hunting Ministry

I've put you in a peculiar place
Where others may not go.
These are My children too
And I want them to know

They may have a rough exterior
But I look into their heart.
I'm standing at the door
I want to give them a new start.

As you share your life with them
And ground them in My word,
You have the words of life
That they may have never heard.

I will give you favor in their sight
As you share camaraderie.
In little subtle ways
You can introduce them to Me.

As you plant and others water
I will cause them to grow.
As you are obedient to My voice
You will reap what you sow.

RECHARGE

You have stayed the course
In spite of hardship and distress.
Now is the time to step aside
For restoration and for rest.

Just get back in the boat
You can walk on water later.
Your battery needs recharging
For the task will be greater.

I will fill you up anew
This time will not be wasted.
Enjoy this season with your family
Of My blessing you have tasted.

When the timing is just right
I will launch you once again.
My anointing will be on you
Many souls you will win.

You've grown in depth and maturity
By the things that you've been through.
Relax and let Me soothe the hurts
And wait for something new.

You know My calling on your life
A special one you see.
I'm sending you after My lost sheep
To bring them back to Me.

Don't worry about your future
I hold it in My hand.
Don't try to figure it out
But it will be something grand.

Send Me

On the surface you appear calm
But I see your heart's desire.
You're tired of seeing lukewarm
"Lord, set their hearts on fire."

Many in My body are bound
You want to see them set free.
I hear the cry of your heart
Lord, why don't you send me?

To you the path seems crooked
With no clear view in sight.
Just let Me lead you step by step
Then everything will be alright.

I have placed these gifts in you
I know just what I want to do.
Be still and listen to My voice
And then you follow through.

I'll use you in a powerful way
My children to set free.
As you obey and follow My will
You bring glory and honor to Me.

STAFF

You are the glue behind the scenes
That keeps things from flying apart.
You are efficient and capable,
You have wisdom and are also smart.

You are always thinking of others
Helping in any way you can.
Keeping things running smoothly
So they don't get out of hand.

You may not feel appreciated
For all the things you do.
But I, your Lord, am always watching
And I am so proud of you.

You've studied to advance your education
So you are prepared to answer My call.
I'm preparing the path before you
Listen to My voice; you can't do it all.

Just be obedient as you listen to Me
I will guide and direct your feet.
Then together we'll accomplish so much
And our journey will be Oh so sweet!

I AM
SPEAKING

To My Pastors

ATTENTION

A PRETTY FACE

The time and money spent on painting the face
What a terribly sad façade.
Neglecting the heart of the believer;
This is of utmost importance to God.

People are not drawn to pretty buildings
But to the peace and joy they see in us.
They want what we have found
In someone they can trust.

Country Clubs are inviting
They are beautiful and comfortable too.
But they can never fill that empty spot inside
Something only Jesus can do.

We who are Spirit-filled believers
We can worship most anywhere.
We are happy and fulfilled
Just as long as the Holy Spirit is there.

It could be a warehouse or someone's home
When we worship and love as one.
Things will begin to happen
God's will on earth will be done.

We must be good stewards of our resources
Money spent growing disciples, helping those in need.
Not wasting money on foolish embellishments
This is basically wasting God's seed.

The Church will stand accountable
For money wisely or unwisely spent.
So, each pastor must be careful
Of the things he may have to repent.

He is the shepherd of the flock
So, the burden rests at his feet.
The decisions he makes must be wise
So the end won't be bitter, but sweet.

PRAYER

I have called and anointed you
To lead this corporate prayer
You won't have to do it alone
For I will always be there.

I'll show you the things that are important
Those that weigh heavy on My heart.
Then I'll give you the words to say
That power, in prayer, will impart.

The things in the world are getting worse
But I control the future events.
Your prayers will have an impact
And bring relief when things get tense.

I will take care of My children
When they put their trust in Me.
There are many souls in bondage
That I want to see set free.

So be faithful to pray as I lead
I will send others to stand by your side.
You will expose many plots of the enemy
He'll have no place to hide.

Revival only comes through ardent prayer
As you seek My way, and My will.
You will grow in your faith and trust
As your heart's desire, I fulfill.

Don't consult with others
They will lead you astray.
Just seek My face and My wisdom,
And I will show you the way.

DRY CRUMBS – FRESH BREAD

Out of my own intellect and resources
I can only offer others dry crumbs.
My words without Your anointing
Are just like beating drums.

It's a sound without meaning
Empty to change the situation.
Only the Holy Spirit
With His intervention

Can turn things around.
Give them Jesus- the Bread of Life.
Then they will be empowered
For His presence will suffice.

MAKE DISCIPLES

God said to go and make disciples
Not just to go save men.
It's the Holy Spirit's work
That draws them unto Him.

The world is filled with spiritual babes
Who don't even know that this is war.
They drift through life just like the World
Not even knowing what we are fighting for.

We cry out to you, Lord
Tell us just what it will take.
What must we do
To get these children to awake?

Men like you who are willing
As they give their very all
To teach, to work, to pray
In answer to My call:
TO RAISE UP DISCIPLES.

My Altar

My altar is a sacred place
Where I will meet with men.
When they confess and ask forgiveness
I will cleanse them of all sin.

If you are ashamed of Me before men
You don't know Me or My Father.
When you fill your church with people
Who haven't changed, why bother?

At the altar you are close to My heart
And your worship is like sweet incense.
Just bask in My presence
And you will drop off every offence.

There you will find new strength and joy
So you can face the day ahead.
For in My very presence
Your spirit has been fed.

MY PASTORS CHOOSE

When pastors get serious about prayer
That's when you will have revival.
When you seek My face instead of My hand
That one ingredient is vital.

The key to signs, wonders, and miracles
Is asking, knocking, and seeking.
Yet very few pastors will invest this time.
What you have not sown, you won't be reaping.

Prayer is that vital connection
Like a pipeline for the Holy Spirit's gifts.
It's the rudder that drives the ship
No wonder My Churches are adrift.

Signs, wonders, and miracles
Are just waiting to be used.
But prayer must become a priority
And My pastors are the ones who choose.

My Shepherds

The sheep don't belong to the shepherd
Nor the shepherd to the sheep.
They all belong to Me – their Father
And they are Mine to keep.

I know which pasture to put My sheep in
So they continue to grow.
Sometimes the shepherd wants to keep them
Or the sheep refuse to go.

I know My sheep better than they know themselves
And I know where they need to be.
Some are hard-hearted and refuse to move
As a result, they never get free.

I've given each shepherd different gifts
I expect him to use them with care.
Many sheep are burdened with problems
I'll be with you, the burden to share.

If My sheep listen to My voice
And go where I tell them to go.
Then they will reach maturity
And avoid much sorrow and woe.

My shepherds should never feel bad
When I move My sheep elsewhere.
I will send you other sheep
Who need your nourishment and care.

This is what I expect from My shepherds
To woo each sheep and win his soul.
To raise him to maturity
That should be My shepherd's goal.

PASTORS

Pay attention to your spouse and children
That's where the next attack may come.
You are so busy with the church
Of your time, they barely get a crumb.

You are their spiritual covering
God put them in your care.
The frustration of being a pastor
Will be lightened if you let them share.

The enemy is subtle and sneaky
He may slip up on your blind side.
Keep a prayer covering over your family
Let the Holy Spirit be your guide.

Set aside time with each one individually
Let them know how precious they are to you.
When you put things in proper order
God will take you through.

Whatever the trials and testing
You will triumph in the end.
God will use you to bring him glory
And on His faithfulness, you can depend.

RESTORE

Lord there are so many spiritual babes out there
That really don't have a clue
That this is spiritual war we are in
And they have to learn to depend on You.

The battle won't be won with missiles or guns
But as we stand in the gap and pray.
The enemy's time is growing short
So many conflicts are coming our way.

The battlefield is our mind
Satan's tactics are deception and lies
We must depend on the Holy Spirit's guidance
To reveal all truth, to make us wise.

We must guard the babes in our care
Snatch them out of the enemy's hand.
Gird their loins with truth
Teach them how to stand.

There are too many pastors still in grave clothes
And time is growing short.
How do we make them understand?
This is war, not a vacation resort.

It's time Your people get serious
Start to recognize the enemy's lies.
Depend on the Holy Spirit's power
Cut loose all demonic ties.

Only as Your children repent and pray
Can You heal our nation once more.
We cry out to You for mercy
For Your name's sake, America restore.

TRAINING GROUND

I've anointed and equipped you
To perform multiple tasks in life.
This is your training ground
And your best support is your wife.

You must listen closely to My voice
I will lead you in the right direction.
Satan will try to interfere
But My Holy Spirit will be your protection.

Don't spread yourself too thin
And weaken your body's defenses.
Guard your mind above all things
Against distraction and offences.

I'm preparing you for greater things
Even beyond your imagination.
Things that you speak and accomplish
Will have an impact on this generation.

The hardships and trials that you've been through
Helped prepare you for the task ahead.
Many others would falter and fall
On this path that you must tread.

I'll lead and guide you each step of the way
Keep focused on each task you see.
Then just do your very best
And leave the rest to Me.

I AM
SPEAKING

To My Pastors

WARNING

BOUNDARY STONE

God's word is the boundary stone
That is being moved today.
If preachers teach a different word
Many children are led astray.

These are spiritual children
And there are many of them out there.
They sit in pews every Sunday
Putting their lives in the Pastor's care.

God is the defender of the faith
A God of ultimate power and wrath.
When anyone leads a child astray
Or directs them on the wrong path

They'll stand before the final Judge
And give account to Him.
He sees all – He knows all
And He has the right to condemn.

So be careful with God's Word
For we know that it is true.
It remains steadfast forever
And to it all honor is due.

Clowns & Goats

There are preachers in the pulpit
That I have not called.
The word that goes forth
Has effectively been stalled.

Like clowns pretending to be someone else
Their messages come from their heads.
Their spirits are far from Me
And the words they preach are dead.

There are people in church pews
They are as lost as a goose.
Satan has them lassoed
And he is tightening the noose.

They pretend to be someone they're not
The enemy has blinded their eyes.
He can be very convincing
And they have listened to his lies.

I will expose the clowns
Separate the goats from the sheep.
There will be purity in My House
And the price they pay will be steep.

COMFORTABLE

Are we supposed to make people comfortable?
When they are on their way to hell?
That's just the way things are
Oh Well!

Aren't pastors suppose to step on their toes
To make them wake up and repent?
Pastors have been called and ordained
And then they are sent

To the lost sheep wherever they are
They're to bring them back into the fold.
To minister salvation to them
To disciple them and make them bold.

It's sheep that begat sheep
So, are we doing our job?
Or are we helping the enemy
From other's salvation to rob?

The Pastor is failing in his calling
If he's not equipping the people to go out.
To witness God's love for everyone
That banishes all fear and doubt.

Our Church should be growing
The members filled with purpose and zeal.
Then people will take notice
No pretending, it's time to get real.

The end times are drawing closer
The windows of opportunity will shut.
It's time to get up and start moving
We must hoist ourselves out of our rut.

Fat Sheep

I'm separating the sheep from the sheep
Instead of feeding My sheep, they feed off My sheep.
Now the time of reckoning has come
What they have sown, they will now reap.

I turn a blind eye just so long
To give them time to repent.
But instead of turning back to Me
They pillage, plunder, and prevent

My sheep from standing on their feet
Depending on My care.
They exalt themselves instead of Me
Hypocrisy I will not bear.

The end is looming way too close
To waste time on errant shepherds.
My sheep are very precious to Me
And your deeds are in My records.

Those who've taken advantage of My sheep
Eternal judgment will face.
You have taken advantage of My calling
And forfeited My mercy and grace.

ICHABOD

How sad when we see written over a Church
The name Ichabod.
Everything is man's ideas and plans
They have lost the presence of God.

It breaks the heart of the Father
He loves each church as His own.
But He is forced to turn His back
If man is seated on the throne.

The Pastor holds the responsibility
He is the shepherd of the flock.
When he stops listening to the Holy Spirit
Salvation and growth will come to a stop.

God always has a remnant
That keeps the flame bright and alive.
With their prayers and intercession
They may help the church survive.

But only if the pastor will humble himself
Repent and be filled again
Allowing the Holy Spirit to move freely
Then healing can begin.

God is the author of another chance
So, let's pray like never before.
Cry out for God's mercy and grace
And pray this Church He'll restore.

My Presence

You don't welcome My presence
You have programs instead.
That's why My children
Are not being fed.

You have fellowship and entertainment
No Holy Spirit revival.
That is what My children will need
To ensure their survival.

You don't let the Spirit
Come and fill His role.
Things may be different
You might lose control.

People get antsy.
If the service runs over an hour
So, there is no revival
No evidence of power.

If some people choose to leave
They weren't hungry at all.
Their ears are closed
They don't hear My call.

What happened to radical transformation
Where bondages were removed?
Miracles so unmistakable
That scoffers could not remain unmoved.

You are supposed to be a peculiar people
Not just like those around.
You could look at someone and see My glory
Where now, can they be found?

Until you truly hunger and thirst for Me
Neither hot, nor cold, you will remain.
Ask Me to light the fire within you
Then stand and make it plain.

NEGLECTED PRAYER

It's going to take persecution
To put My children on their knees.
They are conceited and self-centered
And always do as they please.

They think this time of prayer
Is something that is not needed.
That's why things are so bad
And nothing for you has succeeded.

When will you wake up from your stupor?
Realize I meant what I said about prayer.
When you neglect this important command
Then you wonder why I am not there.

I am not speaking to the world
But to those that I call Mine.
You have failed in your mission
And civilization continues to decline.

Yet you sit back and blame Me
When you have not sought My direction.
You will suffer the consequences
For you have forfeited My protection.

WARNING

STUBBORNNESS

Stubbornness is of the devil
It is not a godly trait.
To impose your will on others
To bow to what you dictate.

This will lead to destruction
If it is not turned around.
In a pastor it is devastating
He is treading on dangerous ground.

A teachable humble spirit
In God's sight is a special trait.
To listen to other's input
And then for God's answer, just wait.

Each Church belongs to the Lord
He is the Chief Shepherd in charge of them.
He grieves when His children are spiritually hungry
And their cry rises up to Him.

If the pastor repents and humbles himself
Healing can begin to take place.
If he continues in his stubborn way
Then his influence, God will erase.

Generosity and help for the community
Will never take the place of spiritual meat.
Unless a church is winning and discipling souls
It will continue to be spiritually weak.

A Church that was to be a light on the hill
Has become just a shadow now.
Unless its members pray hard and repent
That it can be redeemed somehow.

THE JEZEBEL SPIRIT

The Jezebel spirit is subtle
It always comes in disguise.
Often, it's hard to detect
Unless one is really wise.

The individual is very charismatic
The gifts are operating in many ways.
And since God's gifts are without repentance
Most people will stand amazed.

But if the Jezebel spirit is in residence
Many who are vulnerable are led astray.
They don't recognize manipulation and control
And they are easily led the wrong way.

Instead of following God, they follow the leader
Pastors need to take control.
Unless this spirit is recognized and stopped
It will destroy the church's goal.

To My Children

ENCOURAGEMENT

A GODLY MAN

You are the priest of your home
God has assigned you this roll.
You must lead and guide by example
With love and wisdom – never control.

Satan's goal is to destroy your family
With arguments, discord, and strife.
He will tempt you with other women
God expects you to be true to your wife.

Guard your heart with all diligence
So the words you speak will be wise.
Let truth be your constant companion
Never resort to lies.

Let prayers and praises be upon your lips
That comes from a pure, undefiled heart
God has anointed and chosen you.
From His guidance never depart.

Strength and bravery are your attributes
So, guard your household with care
God has given you a godly wife
She will encourage you with love and care.

As you lead, your children will follow
So be careful the path that you take.
Your family will be strong and secure
As you encourage each one to participate.

You should always be rich in mercy
And give generously to the poor.
God will bless you and your family
Like you've never been blessed before.

A GODLY WIFE

Her price is above rubies
She's your helpmate, your queen.
In matters of your household
She reigns supreme.

She's the cook, the chauffer
The housekeeper, the nurse.
She honors her marriage vow
For better, or worse.

She loves and cares for you
Honors you in all her ways.
Brags about you and the children
At other men, she won't even gaze.

She comforts and consoles you
When things around go wrong.
Her faith is deeply rooted
When you are weak, she is strong.

She is active in her church
Serves in the community as well.
With energy and enthusiasm
If she's tired, you can't tell.

She puts up with your hobby.
Fishing, hunting, golf, or something else.
She rejoices when you invite her along
Or she is content by herself.

When the day's activities are over
She is still there by your side.
What God has joined together
Let no man divide.

A HEAVY ANNOINTING

When you have a heavy anointing on your life
You must drink the cup that Jesus drank.
Sometimes it will be sweet
Sometimes it will be rank.

When it is sweet, drink it with gratitude.
When bitter, drink it with His grace.
Others will be watching.
So, drink it with a smile on your face.

Your life will reflect Jesus' glory
Things in this world you will change.
Warn of troubles to come
Sinners to Saints exchange.

Just as Jesus looked beyond the cross
And saw what the future would bring.
Look beyond this present pain
And then your very soul will sing.

The price you pay will be worth it all
You've fulfilled your destiny as well.
Shared the Gospel with all who would listen
And saved many souls from hell.

AGING

We may be older in physical years
But our spirits are renewed day by day.
Our love for Jesus has grown deeper
And we understand more clearly His way.

Wisdom comes with maturity
As we weather the storms in life that come.
We've studied and meditated on God's word
It's exciting and never humdrum.

Simeon and Anna in the Bible
Were filled with expectation.
They believed the promise God had given them
And they received a divine revelation.

Youth may be filled with zeal
But they can be easily led astray.
By the cares of this world
And different doctrines that come their way.

Middle Age is just a stepping stone
Setting deep spiritual roots or following their peers.
Too many choose to believe new doctrine
The old is dull to their ears.

New ideas and revelations are exciting
They stir them up to follow.
If they aren't based on God's word
They are worthless and hollow.

Don't look down on those with grey hair
If they are Christians, their roots are deep.
They have seen and experienced many miracles
Now what they've sown, they are ready to reap.

ALL VETERANS

I know the trouble you went through
The burdens that you shared.
Many on the battlefield were killed
Somehow your life was spared.

War leaves men with scars
Physically and mentally as well.
You may look alright on the outside
But any kind of war is Hell.

Things you've seen will stay with you
Life will never be the same.
The time that was lost with family
You can never regain.

Some were prisoners of war
Many have Post Traumatic Syndrome.
Some lost arms and legs
But they were glad they made it home.

There are those homeless and without jobs
Our government doesn't seem to care.
Many continue to commit suicide
With no one their burdens to share.

For many there are nightmares and flashbacks
Some things are hard to forget.
You have served your country with honor
And all who live are in your debt.

Only a personal encounter with Jesus
Will help you forget the past.
He will renew your mind
And you'll be totally free at last.

BUT GOD

I would have been lost
But God intervened.
I was blinded by the world
Things were not what they seemed.

The Holy Spirit drew me
But God was behind it all.
I made Jesus Lord of my life
Now He's my all in all.

Life has taken on new meaning
Each day is a new adventure.
But God is working on me
Helping me to grow and mature.

My passion may begin to grow cool
But God comes and reignites the flame.
It's burning brighter than ever
And it illuminates His name.

I can't do everything
But God empowers me to help one.
As we each fulfill our part
His will on earth will be done.

You may have turned your back on Jesus
But God loves you just the same.
He will continue to draw you to Himself
Until the end of your life's game.

DAILY PRAYERS

The Holy Spirit takes our feeble prayers
And turns them into something great.
They go straight to the throne of God
And results they then create.

When we pray in the Spirit
It is so power-filled.
That the enemy is overwhelmed
And his venom is distilled.

God hears our every prayer
And the answer is on its way.
As we wait in confidence
It will not delay.

If it involves another person's will
The time may not be right.
But God is true to His promises
Though they are hidden from our sight.

Don't grow weary in waiting
Things will turn out right in the end.
The Holy Spirit is working in their lives
And the answer lies around the bend.

Our patience and persistence
Help us to grow strong.
We've passed the test of time
And we know to God, we belong.

OPTIMISM

Let's not be like Chicken Little, crying
The sky is falling, the sky is falling.
Our gospel is not about gloom and doom
That is definitely not our calling.

Even when things are dark and forbearing
We are not to complain and whine.
The darker the world around us becomes
The brighter we are to shine.

The end may be around the corner
That is not to be our concern.
We are to be busy making disciples
Not worrying about Jesus' return.

When we see that night is coming soon
We must work harder while it is day.
If this is the last generation
We must be on watch and pray.

We can still be filled with joy
In the midst of tribulation.
We can look up and see Jesus
What a glorious revelation.

This world is filled with beauty and opportunity
And if we aren't locked up in prison.
There are too many pessimistic people
We should be filled with optimism.

Our God is a God of joy and hope
We've all read the end of the story.
Jesus comes back as Lord and King
Arrayed in splendor and glory.

EMBRACE THE PLACE
Ecclesiastes 3:5

There is a time to embrace
And a time to refrain from embracing.
Whatever the season in our lives
God knows what we are facing.

When we are first born again
As babes we need lots of care.
Everything is sunshine and roses
And God answers our every prayer.

Then we grow and reach adolescence
It's a time to lay down some rules.
We are reckless and uninhibited.
And we sometimes act like fools.

Our God is patient and caring
And He gives us a lot of slack.
When we get ourselves in trouble
He gently leads us back.

Then we move on toward maturity
Tests and trials we now must face.
Jesus is interceding for us
And we become strong in His grace.

Now we've come to the place of dying
To all of our self-interests and care.
It has taken much time and effort
But it all was worth going there.

For now, comes our resurrection
We have counted the cost.
We're seated in Heavenly places with Jesus
And we don't even miss what was lost.

EVIL

If God is good
Why does evil abound?
The Garden of Eden was perfect
Yet evil in it was found.

Man wants to be like God
To control his circumstances.
To do things his own way
And have whatever he fancies.

God gave man free choice
To love and serve Him on his own.
If love is forced – it is not real
Pretension God will not condone.

How would we recognize good
Where no evil does exist?
There must be opposites for comparison
Or there is nothing to resist.

Trials and hardship bring perseverance
And that tends to build character in us.
Those who are petted and pampered
Just sit around and rust.

God desires that we walk in health
While on earth, Jesus healed everyone.
Choices and circumstances interfere
And the victory can't always be won.

God brings good out of suffering, even death
When the burdens with Him we share.
As we continue to love and serve Him
We can minister to others – for we've been there.

We may not see the good for many years
Sometimes only time will tell
How many have come to know Jesus
And others who have been saved from hell.

So, it pays to keep on keeping on
Whether healthy or crippled in some way.
Our time on earth will be well spent
And eternity will bring a better day.

Jesus is the answer to evil and suffering
He took them willingly.
Ours will last only for a season
For in Heaven, we'll be set free.

ENDING – BEGINNING

When there is an ending, there is a beginning
Of something, that's entirely new.
There is no retirement in God's army
No one should be just sitting on a pew.

There are needs all around us
And God has something special for you.
He wants to involve all of His children
Not just a chosen few.

Ask God to show you your place
Then wait, and the answer will come.
It may be ministering to the poor and needy
Or maybe a song that needs to be sung.

You'll find such joy and fulfillment
That He's chosen you for a special task.
But you can't just sit around waiting
He tells us to simply, ask!

JARS OF CLAY

We are jars of clay
We have God's fire inside.
Only when we have been broken
Can it be seen far and wide.

Just like Gideon's army
Who routed the enemy,
We will be victorious
When our fire others can see.

So, don't refuse to be broken
It's the only way to win.
Light always prevails over the darkness.
And it reveals evil and sin.

Only as light reaches the problem
Can healing begin to take place.
The enemy hidden in darkness is exposed
And now God extends His grace.

You are a new creation
You have God's fire inside you.
Another light to expose the darkness
To both the Gentile and the Jew.

KNOCKED DOWN

When you get over one thing
And another knocks you down,
You think that you are moving forward
And then you're losing ground.

It's easy to get discouraged
And you ask God, why?
He may not answer
But He is always standing by.

He weeps when you hurt.
He understands it all.
You will make it through somehow
Remember His servant Paul.

When this trial is behind you
The mystery will unfold.
You've been through the fire
And come out pure gold.

LITTLE THINGS

God is into details
Pay attention to the little things.
It may seem insignificant
But a mighty outcome it brings.

When Jesus told Peter to let down his nets
Peter only let down one.
The catch was overwhelming
So, others had to get the job done.

When Jesus speaks, listen closely
So you understand each word.
You may be surprised by what you hear
It seems absolutely absurd.

Jesus knows what He wants to accomplish.
If you really want to be included,
Step out in faith without hesitation
Or you will be excluded.

God is more powerful than we think
Nothing is impossible with Him.
We say this quite often
But our understanding is dim.

If we really believe with all of our heart
No endeavor will be too large.
We'll move in with courage and determination;
We'll know that it is God who is in charge.

So, gird up your loins of faith
Do mighty works in His name.
Be they big or little doesn't matter
You've just ignited a flame.

A flame that will spark revival
In someone God put in your path.
Another soul for His Kingdom
Who has been saved from Satan's wrath.

LOVE

Love should give wings to the feet of service
And strength to the arms of labor.
God is love and we His children
Have been blessed with His favor.

Love stands alone in its power
You can't fight it with your words or action.
It gives no weapon to the accuser
This brings us satisfaction.

To the accusers of the woman caught in adultery
Jesus said, "He without sin cast the first stone."
They all turned and walked away
And left Jesus and the woman alone.

God in His love has forgiven us
For we all have sinned and fallen short.
We try all of the worldly things
And find love as a last resort.

REAL FRUIT

Buds and blossoms are not fruit
They are just for show.
It's not by our eloquent words others see
But by our actions they will know.

Paul said that faith without works is dead
This saying is certainly true
Words are cheap – actions costly.
Which one describes you?

It's easy to talk and dream big dreams
But they are only pie in the sky.
Unless they are coupled with good deeds
Those words will simply die.

Fruit is produced with patience and love
As long as we stay connected to the vine.
This vine is Jesus, who nourishes us
So others may come and dine.

As others partake of the fruit we produce
They will grow and flourish too.
This orchard will be pleasing to God
For we have followed through.

SCARS

Don't hide your scars
They're signs of the victories you have won.
This is all a part of your story.
And it has just begun.

There will be other battles ahead
But you'll grow stronger in every skirmish.
God may turn up the heat
For He's refining you in His furnace.

You will come through in victory
Like burnished silver and gold.
God will look down with pleasure
And the world will behold

Another of God's masterpieces
That has been tried and found to be true.
So always look forward to your battles
For God is so proud of you.

STORMS

Father, everything is filtered through Your loving hands
Nothing comes of which God is not already cognizant.
The things that befuddle us in our lives
They didn't just happen by chance.

His mercy is concealed in every storm cloud
His grace flows behind each crosscurrent.
We have His wisdom in every perplexity
So the things that come are not a deterrent.

If it weren't for the winds of adversity
We would grow soft and dull.
When winds are high, and waves are thundering
We tend to seek a peaceful lull.

It is in times of strain and stress
That we can see Jesus most clearly.
This is our heart's desire
So, we welcome the storms sincerely.

God does not promise to make us strong
He is our strength when we are weak.
When we realize our own helplessness
His grace is what we seek.

God created us to glorify Him
So, let God be God – let man be man.
We don't have to perform miraculous feats
Just release them into God's mighty hand.

God uses the simple to confuse the wise
So be slow to interrupt.
We only must always stay humble
For God is the one who will lift us up.

TASTE

God is never wasteful
There's enough anointing for the task ahead.
Now whatever the assignment
Move with confidence, even if it's to raise the dead.

As long as we keep giving out
There will always be an abundant supply.
The gifts will quickly stop flowing
If we're fearful and don't even try.

The power of the Almighty God
Is behind our every endeavor.
He just needs a willing vessel
We don't even have to be clever.

He even used a donkey
So why do we think He can't use us?
We are more valuable than the sparrows
But willingness is a must.

We'll stand back in amazement
When the impossible takes place.
Now we'll crave to be used
For of God's power, we've had a taste.

TEACHERS

Called, anointed, and equipped
A teacher is all of these.
When I give you this position
You accomplish it with ease.

You are guiding and shaping lives
No matter the age or sex.
I give you patience and wisdom
To persevere when you are vexed.

You may not see the results on earth
But the seeds that you plant and nourish
I will not let them lie dormant
For one day they will bloom and flourish.

You won't receive many accolades from men
But your rewards will come from above.
For you have studied and given your time,
And you have done it out of love.

THE ANOINTING

When the power fails
The anointing flows.
As the Holy Spirit moves
So, our Spirit grows.

Joy bubbles to the surface
It cannot be contained.
It breaks forth like the sunshine
Peace is now sustained.

We can rest in the anointing
And just let the Spirit have his way.
Those around will be blessed
Like the dawning of the day.

Light will break forth
Illuminating us from within.
When His anointing is flowing through us
It will draw women and men.

Now their ears are open to the Gospel
We can share and win their soul.
Then, the Spirit will begin His work in them
To cleanse and make them whole.

The Banquet Table

The Lord has prepared a banquet table
He invites us to sit and eat.
The time that we spend there with Him
Is fulfilling as well as sweet.

There are all kinds of food on the table
Some people want to pick and choose.
They don't realize they are all for our benefit
So, there is nourishment that they will lose.

Many of the dishes are simple
They are easy to digest.
Others take more time to chew
How much time do you want to invest?

The ones we must chew on the longest
Are the ones that will cause us to grow.
They bring nourishment to all of our being
And our ministry begins to flow.

The dessert will follow the meal
A delight God has in store.
We'll find new insight into His Word
And it makes us hungry for more.

So, don't refuse the invitation
To sit at His table and dine.
You'll begin to bear much fruit
You've connected to Jesus – The Vine.

THE BEST

When we walk with God
The best is yet to come.
We've learned of His generosity
So, we won't settle for a crumb.

We sit daily at His banquet table
Tasting all the good things He provides.
He renews our strength day by day
And the Holy Spirit always guides.

We view life expectantly
Waiting to see what God will do.
It will always be a surprise
And it's something entirely new.

When we've walked for years with Jesus
We may be old and grey.
He gives us wisdom and understanding
And He hears us when we pray.

He uses us in powerful ways
That we hadn't really expected.
We've learned some things in life
They have proved to be effective.

Now is not the time to retire
The last lap is the hardest in the race.
But with His help we will finish
And see Him face to face.

THE FATHER'S LOVE

His love is like the ocean
It comes in waves and waves.
It washes away all sin and doubt
And it cleanses us always.

Sometimes it's calm and soothing
Like a gentle lap upon the shore.
Other times the waves are boisterous
Causing our spirits to soar.

Its depths are quiet and deep
Penetrating deep within our soul.
Assuring us that God is there
And He desires to make us whole.

When storms come and billows roar
We stay calm deep within.
His love comes and protects us
And we owe it all to Him.

Many times, we don't see the depth
We only see the calm above.
But as big and deep as the oceans
They are but a touch of our Father's love.

THE FIRST CHRISTMAS

When we reflect on that first Christmas
It was not filled with joy and fun.
Each participant was troubled in some way
Until they witnessed the birth of God's Son.

When Mary found that she was pregnant
She didn't understand.
How could this be possible?
She had never known a man.

Joseph felt betrayed
He had always lived a good life.
Now he felt like a fool
She was pledged to him as his wife.

The Shepherds were terrified
When the angels appeared in heaven.
They were confused and disoriented
Until the good news was given.

The Wise Men were exhausted
They had followed after the star.
To see where it would lead them
For they had all traveled far.

Today, many people are confused like Mary
Not knowing what they should do.
Which direction should they take,
Should they try something entirely new?

Many like Joseph have been betrayed
By a loved one or a very close friend.
Now, they feel like a fool
When and how will this nightmare end?

Then, there are those like the shepherds
Who are simply terrified
By death, divorce, or loss of a job
How are they going to survive?

ENCOURAGEMENT

Others are just like the Wise Men
They're exhausted and at the end of their rope.
With no relief or rest in sight
How will they manage to cope?

The answer to it all lies in the stable
Where Jesus Christ appeared on life's scene.
His life an example, His death paid our debt
From all of our troubles He came to redeem.

So now Christmas is one of joy and peace
If you have made Jesus Lord in your heart.
He will walk beside you always
You will never ever be apart.

THE WILDERNESS

The wilderness is a place
We don't want to go.
Yet many times it's the only place
Where God can help us grow.

It's a place of isolation
Of hardship even pain.
We seldom go there willingly
We murmur and we complain.

Jesus came into the wilderness
When He left Heaven and came to earth.
He opened Himself to ridicule and pain
For this is the devil's turf.

If we invite God into our wilderness
And thank Him for His care,
He will share the burden with us
And not give us more than we can bear.

It's in the wilderness that we stop and ask
"God why am I here?"
If we will listen to the Holy Spirit
He will make things clear.

He is molding us and shaping us
For a work He has for us to do.
If we'll just relax and let Him finish
We'll be like someone new.

We will even be surprised
At what He does through us.
He has given us gifts and talents
And put in us His trust.

We'll look back on our wilderness
And thank God for putting us there.
He's done some mighty things through us
And in this world, we've done our share.

ENCOURAGEMENT

When we've done our very best
And finished the work He's given.
We'll enter into His perfect rest
And that will be in Heaven.

WAR

Many of you were so young
You had no idea what war was like.
They sent you off to Boot Camp
And taught you how to fight

Then they sent you all over the world
To places you had never heard of before.
In planes, in battleships or in tanks
To evict the enemy, to win the war.

You saw entire cities destroyed,
Men blown apart – children too.
These horrific memories of war
In your mind, came home with you.

You'll never be quite the same
After seeing man's inhumanity to man.
Your desire to live in peace and harmony
Makes man's greed hard to understand.

God tells us to love and care for each other
As we seek to live together in peace.
If only the world could know Jesus Christ
Then wars like these would quickly cease.

WEIRD

Normal is to look like the world
That's not on God's agenda.
People may call us weird
They are just trying to hinder.

Our walk with the Lord
It's a closer walk as we go.
We're on a spiritual journey
And we will continue to grow

Into the likeness of Jesus
To love as He loves, serve as He serves.
Now there's a place in Heaven
With our name on it, reserved.

Don't let weird bother you
It's a badge of honor you see.
We are representing Jesus on earth
And setting the prisoners free.

Weird is the same as peculiar
We are to be a peculiar people, set apart.
We are walking opposite from the world
For we're following after God's own Heart.

What a privilege to be a servant
Working for Jesus our Lord and King.
It fills our days with wonder
And makes our hearts to sing.

WHY WORRY

Don't worry about tomorrow
God is already there.
He knows our every need
And we are safe in His care.

Worry never accomplished anything
It just wears us out instead.
The energy we have wasted
By our fretfulness and dread.

Most things that we worry about
They will never actually take place.
When trials and hardships do come
We need to seek God's grace.

God sees into our future
Something we cannot do.
No matter what comes our way
He will help us through.

Let no doubt mar our peace
Nor anxieties cloud our brow.
God's grace is always sufficient
He's in the past, the future, and the now.

So much work is waiting to be done
Satan distracts us with worry and care.
So endless time is wasted
When we should be doing our share.

As we minister in the realm of today
We'll have much fruit in the day of reaping.
We have used our time wisely
Not by worrying or sleeping.

Enjoy each moment as it comes
Then joy and peace will fill our day.
We'll be refreshed and ready to face
Whatever comes our way.

WHY?

Don't ask the question "Why?"
Instead "How can I handle this situation?"
"Am I trying to solve it on my own?"
Or "Have I brought God into the equation?"

Many things happen to us in life
That we don't really understand.
But if we trust God to work it out
We'll be a stronger woman or man.

Our faith must be tried by fire
Or we will continue to be weak.
We need to grow in maturity
So, the enemy we can defeat.

God needs strong, tried, and true believers
For there are many children to be led.
We must be strong and know His Word
So that they can be fed.

We don't know the plan for us
That God sees in His mind.
Plans to move us to great things
Let's not be left behind.

The pain or hardship will be forgotten
As we soar to greater heights.
What freedom we experience here
In this our soul delights!

WONDER

Those who are called are loved by the Father
They are kept by Jesus Christ the Son.
What more could we wish for
It has all already been done.

God dwells inside of us
So, we are filled with love and grace.
We want others to have what we have
Peace and joy abound and show on each face.

Godless men try to change this grace
They use it as a license for immorality.
But sin is still sin
And that is a stark reality.

When we've died with Christ
The desire to sin doesn't dwell in us.
The enticements of the world have lost their charm
We view them all with disgust.

Now life is filled with such expectancy
Wondering what God is going to do.
It is always something different
That we didn't expect, but something new.

It could be a divine appointment
So we can share our gifts and talents.
It may be the answer to our prayer
Or that our checkbooks balance.

All good and perfect gifts are from God
And He loves to bestow them on those He calls "Mine."
These moments fill us with wonder
In the midst of life's dull and daily grind.

WORK

When you have to strive for something,
It is always so much better
Than when it's handed to you
On a lovely silver platter.

We know that a person should work
It is commanded in God's Word.
To take credit when handed a fortune
Seems to us a little absurd.

When you work hard for something
Earn it by the sweat of your brow
With no help from others
It's more precious somehow.

Never feel belittled by others
Who think that they are better than you.
They probably would have failed
If they had to struggle – tis true.

You may have started in poverty
And overcome an addiction as well.
You have risen above it all
And now no one can tell.

So, hold your head up high
You are a child of the King.
As such, you will inherit
All the privileges that will bring.

I AM
SPEAKING

To My Children

HIS PROMISES

A Seed

When God plants a seed in your heart
He watches over it with care.
It needs nourishing and protection
Before it can be ready to share.

With the warmth of the Son
And the refreshing of the rain,
It will begin to flourish
And new growth it will attain.

Then leaves and buds will appear
Blossoms spread their sweet perfume.
Your heart will be filled with joy
As their fragrance fills each room.

Then fruit will begin to form
Sometimes it takes time to mature.
Guard against pride and deceit
For the fruit you bear must be pure.

God will use it to nourish others
Either at home or in foreign lands
There will always be a plentiful supply
As you trust it into our Fathers hands.

What started out as a tiny seed
Has multiplied a hundredfold.
Ask God to plant a seed in your heart
In life this should be your goal.

A Thankful Heart

Never get so caught up in the gift.
That you forget the giver.
God not only gives us promises.
But He is swift to deliver.

Only doubt and un-forgiveness.
Keep us from receiving His best.
God loves to bless His children.
Give us peace, prosperity, and rest.

Don't be like the ten lepers.
When only one of them returned.
To thank Jesus for His healing.
It wasn't something he earned.

We are to give thanks for everything.
Even the air that we breathe.
It's the Holy Spirit who draws us to Jesus
So eternal life we receive.

It is essential to give thanks to others.
When they have blessed us some way.
A thankful heart has no room to complain.
So now joy will fill our day.

BRIGHTER

When the darkness seems to overcome
Let our light shine so much brighter
We will not give in to discouragement
For God made us a fighter.

Though the world seems out of control
We know that God is still in charge.
Our finite minds can't see it all.
We know that God's view is large.

He has a master plan in place
That will blow us away.
His plans are beyond our comprehension
But we will understand someday.

We are only responsible for our part
In the area where our influence is shown.
We will let our light shine in the darkness
That God's greatness may be known.

The results are not up to us
We are just to fulfill our role.
God will bring it to pass in His timing
And our blessing will be a hundredfold.

CHAOS

God is a God of order and peace
Chaos and confusion are not on His agenda.
That is Satan's expertise
He wants to disable and hinder.

The plans that God has put in place
To help His children walk in peace
When the enemy brings in confusion
All growth and prosperity cease.

Our thoughts are held captive in disarray
We don't know which way to turn.
Things go steadily downhill
Our minds are blinded to discern.

Now we need to stop and listen
Ask God to show us the way.
To change or get out of the situation
For wisdom and the words to say.

To be able to walk in peace once more
So His will in us can be done.
As we trust Jesus to lead us each day
This battle, we have won.

CONTROL

You will find blessing in any place and every place
When your spirit is in tune with Me.
I will direct every motion of your life
When you release your hold, I will be free

To move you where you need to be
To accomplish My purpose and plan.
Accept each opportunity or roadblock
As coming from My hand.

If there is an obstacle in your path
It is there to help you grow.
Ease and pleasure don't build character
For you face an ancient foe.

You must learn to overcome
For I am depending on you.
There are many who are not prepared
They really don't have a clue.

How to stand against fear and disaster
That are coming in the days ahead.
With My face ever before you
You have no reason to dread.

Man can only kill the body
He cannot touch your soul.
So always walk forward boldly
For you know that I am in control.

DEATH

Death for a Christian
Means Heaven and healing.
Being half alive
Is simply not appealing.

Loved ones may think otherwise
That we should cling to life on earth.
The Bible tells us simply
To celebrate death rather than birth.

This earth in not our home
We're just sojourners here.
No one can live forever
We move closer to death each year.

The Heaven that God has prepared for us.
It will be beautiful beyond belief.
To finally be in the presence of Jesus
What a sweet release.

If we don't have Jesus as our Lord
Then death would be a fearsome end.
We've spent our life doing our own thing
Paying no attention to our sin.

But God loves the sinner too
He's calling – listen to His voice.
Heaven or hell will be our eternity
And until death, we have that choice.

ETERNITY

Eternity is too long to be wrong.
What if the Bible is correct?
You've spent your life doing as you please.
Now everything is a wreck.

You've always done things your way
With no thought for others around.
Now mortality is looking you in the face
With no peace to be found.

You can always turn to Jesus.
The Holy Spirit is calling you near.
Just surrender and say, "I give up Lord."
And now you have nothing to fear

The Spirit will guide you step by step.
Into a life that is filled to the brim.
You're given your heart to Jesus.
And now you belong to Him.

Fear

Life is filled with choices
Sometimes choices bring pain.
We must keep on growing
And learn to trust again.

Some people withdraw into a shell
When they've been molested or abused.
There are those who enjoy seeing pain
They think other people can be used.

When our love has been spurned or rejected
It undermines our self-esteem.
Then we begin to feel worthless
Self-worth is hard to redeem.

God doesn't make mistakes
He understands our feeling of rejection.
If we turn our lives over to him
He points us in a new direction.

Whatever our defense mechanism
God desires to see us whole.
He wants us to have abundant life
To see His plan in our lives unfold.

Love opens us up to hurt
But love is the essence of living.
No matter the past injustices
We must learn to be forgiving.

Then we can begin to heal again
We can enjoy the time that we have here.
Exciting new things are happening
For we've overcome our fear.

GIVE IT AWAY

Time is more precious than money
There are just twenty-four hours in a day.
It's our nature to be stingy with our time
We don't want to give it away.

Mammon is of the world
Time is God's gift freely given.
We need to manage them both wisely
Not frittering them away, or to be success driven.

When we take time from our busy day
Just to spend it with a friend.
We both receive a blessing
For on each other we can depend.

Time spent alone with our Father
It will bless us all through the day.
He gives us strength and wisdom
So we accomplish our tasks without delay.

When someone gives of their time to us
We should receive it with graciousness.
They have chosen to give time away
Instead of using it to feather their nest.

God loves a cheerful giver
Whether it's time, money, or our gifts.
God will reward us openly
As the burdens from our shoulders He lifts.

So always be quick to give
For that saying in the Bible is true.
You can't out give God
For blessings will return to you.

Give it Up

God blesses what He possesses.
Whether it is our money, talent, or time.
It may seem little and unimportant.
But He can make it sublime.

Those things that we hold back
Thinking they are of no use
May be our lack of trust in God.
And we're just looking for an excuse.

When we finally realize
That our Father gives us every possession
And it is nothing we have earned
Then their importance won't be an obsession.

When we take what little we have
And place it in God's hand
We will see that it is multiplied
We can't do it – but God can!

As we freely receive His blessing
Let us freely give in return.
Then in eternity these will be gems
Not wood, hay, and stubble that will burn.

We have laid up treasure in Heaven
Where neither rust, nor the devil can steal.
Our reward will be in eternity
And that, my friend, is a really good deal.

HEARTBREAK

When the worst thing you can think of has happened
And your world has fallen apart.
Know that God was not surprised
He knew about it from the start.

You keep on searching for answers
Yet you may never fully understand.
God knows just what you need
And He already has a plan.

It may not be the answer that you want
But it's one that will be fulfilling.
When you quit struggling and follow Him
And He sees that you are willing.

He will give you new wisdom and insight
And bless you with so much more.
He is taking you in a different direction.
Just walk through it when He opens the door.

The heartbreak will be just a memory
New experiences will bring such pleasure.
You've grown so much closer to Jesus
And you have discovered that hidden treasure.

The knowledge that God has your best in mind
And that He will bless you once more.
With peace, joy and love
Like you've never experienced before.

You will receive appreciation from others
Who have watched you walk through the fire.
You've overcome many obstacles
And obtained your heart's desire.

HELPMATE

Eve was not taken from Adam's head
Or from his feet to be trampled on.
He was not to be lord over her
She was taken from his side to be equal.

They would walk together as one
He was to be her protection.
That's why she was taken from under his arm
So together they would walk in the same direction.

She was taken from close to his heart
God's design was for their good.
She was supposed to be loved
But man has not followed as he should.

Many wives have been abused
They have been lorded over.
She is made to feel inferior
And her husband is often a rover.

God will not be mocked
Each man will reap what he's sown.
If he's unfaithful to the wife of his youth
He will wind up old and alone,

Unless he returns to God's plan
Then God can heal and restore.
When he cherishes the helpmate he's given
Their union will be better than ever before.

HIS VOICE

Death had to lose its hold
And Jairus' daughter had no choice.
She rose up from the dead
At the sound of His voice.

When God gives us a word
It will always be tested.
Will we continue to stand strong?
Or will our faith be arrested?

When God speaks to our circumstances
It will come to pass.
There is power in His voice
But we always have to ask.

Then we can move forward with confidence
Don't dawdle or cause delay.
When God gives us the go ahead
He has already paved the way.

HURT PEOPLE

When someone has maligned or misjudged you.
Just release the problem unto Me.
I know the motives behind the act.
And I will open their eyes to see.

They are only hurting themselves.
When they hurt one of My own.
The act will eventually backfire.
And they will be left alone.

When someone is hurt, they always lash out.
Hurt people, hurt people it is true.
I'm the only one who can heal them.
Cleanse their wounds and make them like new.

Just sit back and watch Me work.
Turn My light on the situation.
Even when you don't understand
My will's manifestation.

I'm working behind the scenes.
To correct and put things in order.
Instead of them doing things on their own.
They must trust Me, whether son or daughter.

I'm preventing trouble in the future.
And protecting those I call Mine.
Trust Me in every situation.
And things will turn out fine.

JESUS WITH SKIN ON

Father, my finite mind cannot comprehend
The depth of Your mercy and grace
The love You show to Your children
For we are a stiff-necked race.

You care about the smallest details
Of the hurts and cares we carry inside
You know our thoughts before we think them
So, there is nothing that we can hide.

You don't reprimand us for our faults and failures
You just help us get back on our feet.
Then, You encourage us to try again
So our failures, we don't repeat.

As we learn and grow in wisdom
We acquire more of Your attributes.
We become more like Jesus
For in Him, we have put deep roots.

Now, we can be Jesus with skin on
To others who are lost and alone.
As we share the Gospel with them
We can lead them quickly back home.

JUST BECAUSE

Just because it's a cloudy day
Does not mean the sun is not there.
Just because you don't feel My presence
Doesn't mean I do not care.

I know every breath that you take
I hear every thought that you think.
I know when you are hungry and thirsty
Then I give you food and drink.

Just because things don't happen quickly
Doesn't mean they won't happen at all.
You may need to grow in maturity
So when it happens, you will not fall.

I know the plans I have for you
To bring glory to My name.
I'm teaching you to be patient
Wisdom and understanding to gain.

When I know that you are ready
To move forward in My plan.
Then obstacles will fall by the wayside
I will lead you by My hand

Into a future filled with joy
Where miracles still take place.
Now relax and let Me take control
Just because of My love and grace.

LISTEN

Shallow streams make the most noise
While the deep are often silent.
The wise man is calm and at peace
While the fool is often violent.

We must train ourselves to listen
To pay attention to each word.
Then we can more readily discern
If it's the truth or just absurd.

Most of the time we listen without hearing.
We are immersed in our own thinking.
When the person talking needs our help
They may be spiritually sinking.

We who are strong must help the weak
This is our Lord's command.
When our brother or sister needs us
To just listen and understand.

Then God will give us the words to say
That will encourage and help them cope.
They will see their rock is Jesus Christ
And that will rekindle their hope.

MOTHERS

I created mothers to be different
For I know that they can bear the pain.
Nine months carrying their child
So a new life they could gain.

Through sleepless nights and endless days
It seemed that things would never get done.
They persevered for love of the child
When a man would probably have run.

A man will brag about his child
A woman holds them close to her heart.
Then she sends them off to school or college
It's so hard for them to be apart.

When a child strays from the truth
And they are caught in Satan's snare,
Others may turn their backs
But a mother will always be there.

She has tried to prepare them ahead
For the hardship in life they will face.
She spends much time in prayer
Asking God for His mercy and grace.

She is sad, yet happy when they marry
Hoping their partner will fill her role.
That they will love and provide for her child
As she sees their lives together unfold.

Then when grandchildren come, what a blessing
They delight her and shower her with love.
The fruit of her womb has flourished
So, she gives thanks to her Father above.

Then, I look down with a smile on My face
At the love they have for each other.
They have pushed through the good and the bad
And I am proud that I made you a mother.

MY SIGNATURE

When we stood on that bluff
With that panoramic view
How could we not sense Your Majesty?
God did it all for me and you.

Every leaf on a tree, every delicate flower
Each one with its unique design.
Things like this can't just happen
This has to be something divine.

Those who are blind to Your wonders
Have cut themselves off from Your light.
Satan has them blinded
We pray God restore their sight.

There are so many wonders around us
Just waiting for us to embrace.
But we must be quiet and still,
Or they are hidden from our face.

God open our eyes to see
The beauty in everything.
Each season will be different
Summer, Fall, Winter, then Spring.

As you walk close beside Me
You will grow and mature.
Then you will recognize
The things that bear My signature.

No Buts

God is a creative being
He doesn't want us stuck in a rut.
When He opens up new avenues for us
All we are constantly saying is: but.

Yes God, that really looks interesting
But I am so busy with something right now.
I know that You will be with me
But I don't really think I know how.

The task ahead seems impossible
And I know that You are able.
But can't You find someone else
Who seems so much more capable?

God I know that You work through me
But my knowledge of Scripture is not great.
And I'm afraid to speak in front of people
Choose someone they'll appreciate.

Do we want to move on with God?
See impossible things take place?
Then we must abandon our buts
And place our trust in God and His grace.

Our Passion

The longer we walk in the Spirit
The greater our passion should be.
We have grown and matured
And our eyes have been opened to see.

The little things that God is doing
They are not just coincidence.
God is working behind the scenes
To orchestrate these events.

The things foretold in the Bible
Are lining up before our eyes.
All we need to do is look around
To recognize the enemy's lies.

Don't ever become complacent
We must keep our passion ever burning.
As the end times draw nearer
We must be even more discerning.

We must depend on the Holy Spirit
Now more than ever before.
He will give us wisdom and insight.
Can't you hear the Lion of Judah roar?

PERSPECTIVE

God doesn't want us to be happy
He wants us to be holy.
Though our circumstances may not change
Our perspective can change boldly.

We know that God works behind the scenes
To accomplish His will in the world.
He is just and sees every motive
One day we will see His will unfurl.

In the meantime, the wicked grow wealthy
The evil seem to win the fight.
We wonder how long it will be
Before we will witness God's might.

God has His own timetable
And we don't know when it will end —
Satan and his minions in the lake of fire
Eden restored like it was back then.

In the meantime, we are to occupy
Bring souls into the fold.
Our reward will be in Heaven
There the streets are paved with gold.

Heaven will come down to earth
It will be the New Jerusalem.
We'll bask in the presence of Jesus
For we owe it all to Him.

REVEALED

Whatever Jesus reveals He heals
Financial problems, or pain of some kind.
It may be fear, pride, or doubt
Or just something troubling our mind.

It must be brought out in the open
So healing can take place.
There is no reason for embarrassment
Others have problems they face.

It takes courage to admit our shortcomings
Yet they are common to man.
Most people don't know Jesus
Or recognize His healing Hand.

But we His followers trust in Him
And know that healing is real.
So, we continue to stand on His Word
No matter how we feel.

It's the Devil who sends pain and weakness
For he comes to kill, steal, and destroy.
He can't plunder our goods
When we don't let him take our joy.

We just rejoice in tribulation
Knowing that we will win in the end.
We praise and worship like never before
For on Jesus, we can depend.

SERVANT

The world detests these words
Servant, obedient, service, and humility.
Our Lord crowned these words
He is the one who gives us this ability.

It is not easy to deny self
We are all selfish to some degree.
In obedience we give up our will
To become what Jesus asks us to be.

His power comes in self-denial
Then we can accomplish great things.
The enemy detests this attitude
And the destruction to his plans it brings.

Only as we become servants to others
Can we lead them to the Cross.
Self-righteousness turns them off quickly
And then our cause is lost.

We can only give out
As we humbly receive.
All else is superficial
And the Holy Spirit will grieve.

So, esteem the title of servant
It is the name Jesus has chosen.
We will be a sweet-smelling savor
And our love will melt those who are frozen.

SMILE

A negative person is hard to be around;
Life's problems, we all have our share.
As Christians we turn them over to Jesus
Then try hard to leave them there.

Smile like everything is fine
Refuse to wear a frown.
We all need to be lifted up
A pessimist will pull us down.

Close friends will lift us up in prayer
But others will never know.
A positive attitude will help us cope
Don't let your troubles show.

God is working on our behalf
We trust Him to show us the way.
There is sunshine behind every cloud
So we thank and praise God each day.

When God sees we are trusting in Him
He comes through for those He calls "mine."
Keep smiling and carry on
And soon the sun will shine.

THE ANSWER

You are being watched!
And what do others see?
Do they see love and compassion?
And are you a reflection of Me?

Do they see judgment and anger
Just like the rest of the throng?
Or do you reach out in mercy to help
Or condemn, what they did wrong?

I am depending on you
To show others the way of the cross.
That My blood covers all of their sin
I don't desire that any be lost.

You are My ambassadors on Earth
I finished the work I came to do.
Will you lay down your life for others?
The answer is up to you.

THE 7 PROMISES OF THE HOLY SPIRIT

Jesus Himself gives us the Holy Spirit
His **presence** in our life is steady.
He will give us the **power** necessary
We just need to be always ready.

Ready His words to speak
Ready His miracles to perform.
Whatever we need He will give us
Even to the quieting of the storm.

He **performs** His work through us
As we have yielded to Him.
It may be something peculiar
We feel we are out on a limb.

He has **positioned** us in the right place
To be used in His **pursuit** of someone.
We'll be surprised at the outcome
When His work through us is done.

The evidence of the Holy Spirit in us
Is our reaction to our pain.
His joy is a constant in our lives
We don't murmur and complain.

Ask:" Holy Spirit what are You saying to them?"
And "What would You have us do?"
To open the door to salvation
So that they may begin to know you.

He often **prevents** us from going somewhere
That He knows would cause heartache.
He is always there to protect us
For His love is real, not fake.

Other's hearts have been **prepared**
Before we are even sent in.
We just open our mouth and witness
Then another soul He will win.

THE WIND
John 3:7-8

No one knows where it comes from
And no one knows where it's going.
It is the same with the Holy Spirit
Whether He is reaping or sowing.

He moves according to the Father's will,
And when we're alive within,
God's will moves us ever forward
Just like He does with the wind.

God has a work for us to do
The Holy Spirit is the wind beneath our sail
As we relax and follow His leading
Our task will succeed, it will not fail.

Only God knows where He is sending us
But the adventure will be fun.
We'll feel as free as the wind
And please both Father and Son.

TIMING

Lord your timing is always a mystery
When we think You will do it, You say "wait."
Then You move when we least expect it
But it's always on time, never too late.

Our finite minds can't understand Your timeline
Yet, it was set in place eons ago.
We just have to wait until we see it happen
Time flies for You, but to us it moves slow.

You are teaching us to be patient
Something that is sorely needed today.
We want it now if not sooner
But You will do it Your way.

It always works out perfect
For Your timing is always best.
If we had obtained it sooner
Our plans would be a mess.

So, we should be content to wait
It will work out best in the end.
For God sees the pitfalls ahead.
He is our Father, Lord, and friend.

YES & AMEN

When God makes you a promise
And you hear it loud and clear
You know that He will answer
If you don't give in to doubt and fear.

For God is not a man
And He does not tell a lie.
So, hold on tight to your promise
Don't ask the question, why?

Though it tarries, wait for it
For it will surely come
When God promises you something
Don't settle for a crumb.

So just wait in wonder and patience
For on God we can depend
For we read in His Word
That His promises are Yes and Amen.

I AM
SPEAKING

To My Children

OUR RESPONSIBILITIES

A BLACK SPOT

When there is one black spot in our lives
It colors everything around.
It captures all of our attention
Peace and joy can't be found.

We forget about all of our blessings
As we concentrate on that one thing wrong.
All of our joy in life has vanished
And we've walked in misery too long.

Look up! For the sun is shining
God is still on His throne.
Things may really be bad in our lives
But He will never leave us alone.

We must run into His arms of love
Shift our burdens into His care.
Things may not change on the outside
But the burden will be easier to bear.

God's peace will fill the empty places
And our faith will rise up once more.
Praises will flow from our heart
And that black spot, we will ignore.

ADVERSITY

Thanksgiving takes the sting out of adversity
No matter the situation.
A tender heart can respond to God's call
No matter the education.

It's the simple that can see clearly
When knowledge often clouds the way.
It doesn't matter about our feelings
We just need to obey.

It may seem impossible and irrational
To be thankful for hardships and pain.
Yet we will be blessed
Though the difficulties may remain.

Thankfulness opens our heart to God's presence.
Then we see things from His perspective.
He will guide us through the maze
For now our heart is receptive.

We will look back on the situation
And realize how much we have grown.
Now we can face adversity with calmness
Knowing we'll never face it alone.

ANGER

A spirit of anger
Is not a good thing.
It can wreak havoc
It's the enemy's sting.

We open the door
Then we let it in
When we don't have our way
Or an argument we don't win.

Righteous anger is different:
When someone's being hurt
Or people are out there
Just throwing dirt.

Calm and clear thinking
Will straighten things out.
A quiet voice of authority
Instead of a shout.

When temper has cooled
Then one can see clearly.
To soothe over turmoil
And apologize sincerely.

A temper tantrum
Never solves anything.
As we seek God's help
His peace it will bring.

BARRENNESS

There is beauty in barrenness
Because we see the true shape.
Everything lies exposed
There is nothing fake.

This is how God sees us
Stripped of our fleshly façade.
He sees the motives behind our actions
For He made us – He is God.

We may fool those around us
Who think we are honest and upright.
But we cannot hide from God
We are naked in His sight.

He desires that we all be holy
And free from all fleshly sin.
When we make Jesus Lord of our life.
This is how we begin

To live a life of holiness.
And bring blessings wherever we go.
We'll be that living epistle
That makes others want to know

What makes our life so full of joy
In spite of the chaos around.
We've discovered that Living Water
And a touch of Heaven, we have found.

BE PATIENT

One moment of impatience
Can rob us of blessing in eternity.
We must learn to wait on God
No matter how long it may be.

Abraham and Sarah were impatient
So, the Arab nation exists.
Now hatred of the Jews and Christians
Brings terrorism into our midst.

God knows what is going to happen
So, He always warns us ahead.
If we don't ask His direction
We may just wind up dead.

So, it pays to be patient
To wait and seek God's plan.
Things will work out in His timing
If we put them in His hand.

We'll be surprised at the outcome
It will be better than anything we dreamed.
God is awesome and powerful
And should be highly esteemed.

BROKENNESS

I know what it is to be broken
I have let my Savior down.
I have grieved the Holy Spirit
And my sorrow is profound.

I thought my faith was stronger
But I know I failed the test.
It's hard to forgive myself
And put the memory to rest.

My Father was quick to forgive me
To reassure me that He loves me still.
He knew beforehand that I would mess up
But He had given me free will.

Now He expects me to get back in the battle
I've learned my lesson and have much more to give.
For out of my brokenness comes strength
To show others how they should live.

CALLING

A person cannot give out
What they have not received.
Our empty vessel has nothing to give
So, don't let yourself be deceived.

It was from the hands of Christ
That the multitude received bread.
Jesus is the Bread of Life
And only from Him can we be fed.

Just like the twelve baskets left over
Service is the salvage of our love shone.
All that we do comes from Him
We can do nothing alone.

Service will be futile and burdensome
Until it springs from an overflowing heart.
A heart that is filled with His love
Only now are we ready to start.

We may not receive gratitude from people
It may be hate in jeers and mocking.
They did this to Jesus
So, it should not be shocking.

There will always be a multitude to be fed.
But the ministers will be few.
Many are called, but few are chosen.
Has God been calling you?

CHILDREN

Each child is a gift from God
And they should be handled with care.
They will be a reflection of you
And the influence that you share.

Did you raise them to know Jesus,
To share His love for them?
Or did they grow up in ignorance
And now their future looks dim?

Unless they encounter Him on their own
Or from the witness of a teacher or a friend
You have failed in your responsibility.
Now, on others they have to depend.

They may be successful in this world
But our stay here is temporary.
Where we spend eternity is the question
And their destination is scary.

Each adult is responsible for their choice
But an early firm foundation is a must.
When things around are falling apart
Only in Jesus can we put our trust.

Just make sure you do your part
Then each prodigal will know the way home.
You raised them to know about Jesus
Then, the decision will be theirs alone.

DECONTAMINATE

How far from God's Word
Have we tended to wander?
We get caught up in worldly things
So that's a good question to ponder.

We must decontaminate our minds
For many times it is filled with clutter.
Do we get serious and pray about issues
Or do we sit around to complain and mutter?

First let's clean up our environment
Surroundings can calm or annoy.
Do we see beauty in and around us
Does relaxing at home bring us joy?

Our spiritual atmosphere is most important
Is it joyful or filled with gloom?
When other people are around us
Do they want to linger or leave too soon?

Satan is the ruler of the airways
So, what do we see or listen to each day?
Do we twitter, text, and stay on the computer
Or do we think on Jesus, the Truth and the Way.

We must avoid so much noise
It is a clamoring in our ears.
Do we ever listen to God's still small voice
That comes to quiet and comfort our fears.

Out of our bellies flows living water
To nourish and comfort a thirsty soul.
Is that stream pure and unpolluted
Will it weaken another or make them whole?

God's Word tells us the answer
Think on things that are of a good report.
Then God can depend on us to be
In the storms of life, a safe, sure fort.

Dependence

Our land is in darkness like never before
Both on the inside and outside as well.
We've left the safety of God's care
Where He tells us to dwell.

War's threatening on many fronts
Our freedom once more we must defend.
On those willing to give their all
We will again have to depend.

We pray God's blessing on those who go forth
May His protection and favor rest on you.
Amid the hardships and dangers ahead
Depend on Him and you'll make it through.

Many who've gone before paved the way
By sacrificing their time and skill.
To thwart the plans of the enemy
Who comes our freedom to steal.

Today, we honor those who are serving now
And those who have served before
We owe our lives and safety to you
We're here to say. "Thank you once more."

DOUBT

When there is doubt – wait
God is in control.
We see through a glass darkly
God always sees the whole.

We may be headed for danger
Or pitfalls we may not see.
Too often we are impatient
To see someone set free.

We may be standing in the way
Of something God wants to do.
The person may need to learn to stand
To depend on God, to see him through.

When we are the enabler
We are taking over God's role.
Instead of helping – we hinder
When we have taken control.

God wants us to completely let go
Of the situation or person in need.
Then God can step in and do His job
And He is the only one who'll succeed.

DRESS REHEARSAL

This time is a dress rehearsal
We're preparing for the big show.
God expects us to be prepared
Don't be complacent, we need to grow.

Into that great performer
We were created to be.
Our audience is the Three in One
And they are waiting to see

All that we've learned
On this stage called earth.
Have we heeded His Voice
Or scorned its worth?

What have we done
With this life we've been given?
Has it brought fruit into the Kingdom
Or has it been gratification driven?

We've each been given a measure of faith
Has yours shrunk, or has it grown?
No one else is responsible
It rests with you alone.

To whom much is given
Much is expected.
Will we be accepted
Or will we be rejected?

Encourage yourself in the Lord as David did
You are stronger than you think.
God is always with you
If you have Jesus that missing link.

The final performance is at the judgment seat
Where our life will pass in review.
Did we win souls and bear fruit?
Will we hear, "Well done, I'm proud of you"?

EXTRAVAGANT GIVING

Extravagant giving should mark us as Christian
We are to give and not to take.
In order to be like Jesus
We are to love, never to hate.

This even includes our enemies
Our prayers are for others.
God made us all
So, we should be sisters and brothers.

When we see a need, we should fix it
For God has blessed us with more.
God gives us the ability to make riches
He expects us to share it with the poor.

If we hoard or spend it on ourselves
It will bind us as sure as chains.
We have riches on earth not in heaven
And we forfeit our soul for gains.

We must give of our time not just our money
People need to know that we care.
We need to take time to listen
For others have a story to share.

When we unselfishly give of ourselves
God will be pleased with us.
Now we are reflecting Jesus
And Satan is filled with disgust.

In eternity we'll have time and riches
When we share what we have on earth.
Our reward will be in Heaven
And this is of infinite worth.

FLYING

We were meant to fly
Not sit on a bench, chirp and make a mess.
When we are soaring like eagles
We are free as we feel the wind's caress

Far above the darkness and gloom
That is so prevalent in our world today.
We just want to keep on flying.
It's a wonderful place to stay.

From this height we can see clearly
The things on earth that we need to do.
Serving, witnessing, teaching, always loving
God will reveal it and we follow through.

We have to come down to minister
Do the things that have to be done.
Then we'll take off and soar again
We are having so much fun.

If you are content just sitting on a bench
You have let the enemy clip your wings.
You've denied yourself the pleasure
That soaring with Jesus always brings.

FOUND

A poured-out life is: blessed, broken, and given away
This is what God wants from us.
A life that we place in His loving hands
With wholehearted worship and trust.

It won't matter where He sends us
Nor the hardships along the way.
He already knows our destination
And the things that will cause delay.

As long as we remain steady and true
He will use us to accomplish His will.
We just pour out our love on others
The naked to clothe, the hungry to fill.

It may be a smile or encouraging word
That people need to see and hear.
Selfishness in this world is the norm
That is filled with hardship and fear.

A getting life is easy, a giving life is hard,
But the rewards will be great.
This is how God meant us to live
And love will always overcome hate.

When we give of ourselves unselfishly
It will impact those around.
Turn their eyes to the Savior Jesus
Now the lost have been found.

GOD'S GENERALS

Precious in the sight of the Lord is the death of His Saints
It is costly when a general has been taken out.
Those whom God has trained through the years
And who know what this war is about.

There are so many young believers
Who are eager to fight but haven't been trained.
They rush in when they see an opportunity
And their faith ends up killed, or maimed.

The older saints in the church must teach the younger,
If we are going to win this fight.
The tactics of the enemy are the same always
But they must be brought to light.

There is no retirement in Gods army
Unless your mind is affected some way.
Even those disabled, or in Nursing Homes
You are still expected to pray.

If you are mobile and in reasonable health
You are needed in the war zone.
To lead and direct the fight against the enemy
Young believers are never to be left alone.

Together we will win this war
If all believers stay in the fight.
We must expose the plan of the enemy
Who are spirits, hidden from our sight.

GRACE

Anger vanishes in the face of grace.
Is this any surprise?
Love shines forth like a sunbeam
While anger is often in disguise.

It is really hard to fight love
When you see that it is real.
A soft answer turns away wrath
No matter what you really feel.

This is important in God's Word
We are to love and forgive our enemy.
To give more than is expected of us.
In this world of evil – that's the remedy.

When we make our enemy our friend
We have pleased the heart of God.
He loved and forgave us as His enemies
When we expected Him to use a rod.

Forgiveness brings friends to us
And foils the enemy's plan.
He caused division and hatred
In order to destroy our land.

When we learn to cooperate with God
Peace will reign in our lives.
It is in this atmosphere
That love and contentment thrives.

GUARD

Guard your mouth with all diligence
For out of it flows the issues of life.
The good man brings forth treasure
A fool brings only envy and strife.

Guard your eyes and what they see
The lust of the eyes leads to temptation,
And if we are not very careful
We are drawn into participation.

We must not envy what we see in others
Their possessions or what God does through them.
Our abilities and ministries are gifts
And they all come from Him.

We must guard our ears always
And the things that we hear.
Satan whispers evil thoughts and ideas
That make things different than they appear.

So be careful the things you hear and repeat
They may not be true at all.
But the damage that they inflict
That will be hard to recall.

Guard your mouth diligently
With it we give the enemy information.
That he will use to undermine our faith
And he does it with justification.

If he can put doubt in our mind
About God's Word or His actions
To make us think He is cruel or unfair
This brings him satisfaction.

So, always be alert and on guard
The enemy seeks to destroy and devour.
We are helpless on our own
So, we must depend on God's power.

HAVE I NAILED JESUS TO THE CROSS?

I nail Jesus to the cross if I say that His sacrifice
was not enough to cover someone else's sin.
I nail Jesus to the cross if I have sex outside marriage.
I nail Jesus to the cross if I put things in my temple that cause me harm.
I nail Jesus to the cross if I gossip and steal someone's good name.
I nail Jesus to the cross if my road rage causes an accident.
I nail Jesus to the cross if I get drunk and act like a fool instead of a Christian.
I nail Jesus to the cross if I take credit for something that He did through me.
I nail Jesus to the cross if I covet things that belong to someone else.
I nail Jesus to the cross if I fail to help the poor.
I nail Jesus to the cross if I think that I am better than someone else.
I nail Jesus to the cross if I have unforgiveness in my heart.
I nail Jesus to the cross if I seek revenge.
I nail Jesus to the cross if I use His name in vain.
I nail Jesus to the cross if I use crude jesting.

How have you nailed Jesus to the Cross?
We do it knowing that it is sin.
Jesus knows our flesh is weak
When we ask, He forgives us again.

As we mature and gain in wisdom
Then sins lose their power.
We've turned our desire toward Heavenly things
To please Jesus who is our strong tower.

HEARTS

There are four different hearts—
Each differs, hearing God's word spoken.
Things in this world have interfered
And three of them are broken.

The **callous heart** has been hardened
And God's word cannot stay.
It's been trodden down by lust and sin
So, the enemy quickly steals it away.

The **careless heart** is superficial
The love of self is the main concern.
It's shallow, so the seed can't take root
So, it withers away, and is brought to ruin.

The **cluttered heart** is filled to the brim
With envy, greed, and worldly things.
So, the Word is chucked out early
Before fruitfulness it could bring.

The **clean heart** receives the Word with joy
It can take root and grows strong.
It produces fruit, 30, 60, 100-fold
And it is filled with His song.

HUMILITY

Without true humility
Nothing else matters at all.
Haven't you read in My Word
That pride goeth before a fall.

Pride caused Satan to be kicked out of heaven
I won't tolerate it in anyone I call Mine.
No matter how much you study and pray
It's just a matter of time.

Maybe you've had great teachers of renown
You've just been blessed indeed.
It doesn't make you better than others
But Satan has planted his evil seed.

You each must have a teachable spirit
Open to other's correction.
If you think you are more spiritual
You're headed in the wrong direction.

I'm the One who sets up order in My Church
Your Pastor is the final authority.
You're totally out of place
When you're filled with superiority.

You may be having success for a time
But until you humble yourself
No matter your potential
I will put you on a shelf.

IRRITANTS

Don't despise those things that irritate you the most
Be it trials, church, or the evils in this world.
It was the tiny grain of sand in the oyster shell
That caused it to create that precious pearl.

When life is a bed of roses
We grow complacent and lazy.
Stuck in our comfort zone
Till something happens that drives us crazy.

Apathy is a disgraceful thing
When we view it from God's perspective.
Lukewarm He spews out of His mouth
His holiness and presence must not be neglected.

The irritating things He always uses
To shake us out of our comfortable rut.
The world is filled with needy people
So, let's get off our lazy butt.

We need to be about our Father's business
There are many needs for us to fulfill.
He wants all of His children busy
Seeking to accomplish His will.

So, be thankful for those irritating things
That sent us to the Father's feet.
There we find our rightful place
And His approval is always sweet.

JEALOUSY

Love is as strong as death
Jealousy as cruel as the grave.
When we give in to this green-eyed monster
That's not the Christian way to behave.

We must be content with what we have
Not covet what others possess.
We may have been lazy in one area
While they worked hard for their success.

God is the one who gives us gifts and talents
What we do with them is up to us.
Many take advantage of what they have
While others let them sit there and rust.

Jealousy causes both big and small problems
Between brethren and nations also.
It must be recognized and brought in the open
Before a friend becomes a foe.

Even wars stem from jealousy
As nation fights against nation.
Instead we uphold one another
When there is success – let's have a celebration!

God is pleased when we love our brother
For Christians are knit together as one.
When we lift up and praise one's success
We are reflecting Jesus – His Son.

LEGACY

When we have been emptied
Of all God has to pour through us.
He will take us home to Heaven
And our body will return to dust.

He designed us each with a purpose
Before earth's foundation was laid.
When we've fulfilled our destiny
Our works will never fade.

They will impact future generations
In a good way or in a way that is bad.
It will be our decision
To act like a saint or to be a cad.

What influence we leave behind
Will be remembered or forgotten.
Those of greatest impact remembered
Whether they are worthy or they are rotten.

What kind of legacy do you want to leave?
It's a good question to consider
One that will make you smile,
Or one that will leave you bitter.

Now is the time to get serious with God.
We must determine to do our share
To leave our country a better place
Because God has planted us there.

LET GO

Why do we want to hold on
To our earthly things so tight?
The hurricanes and tornadoes come
They are blown away like a kite.

Then our lives are devastated
We don't know where to go.
Much that we covet is unnecessary
It's really just a bunch of show.

We want to feel successful in life
And too many times it's judged by wealth.
While true riches are not found in things
But in giving to others and denying self.

God loves us and wants to bless us
With health, peace, and joy.
These are the things the enemy
Seeks to come and destroy.

As long as our faith stands strong,
No matter the losses we've sustained,
We will recover and be stronger
For God's blessings have remained.

Only those things that God gives to us
Are the ones that we really need.
So, let's be satisfied with little things.
And be kind in thought and deed.

OUR RESPONSIBILITIES

LIFE'S STORY

If Jesus is telling His story though your life
What kind of story will it tell?
Will it be one of gratitude and praise
Or that life is a living hell?

If you've turned your back on Jesus' salvation
Then Satan is controlling your actions.
You've allowed your life to become callused
By all this worlds' distractions.

Sinful habits, attitudes, and desires
Are generational curses passed down in a family line.
If you've been born again
These are broken and left behind.

The things that have been done to you
Ridicule, hurts, abuse, all affect your soul.
But the precious blood of Jesus
Will heal and make you whole.

Those things you have done to yourself
Bad decisions, wrong choices, you reap what you've sown.
Sometimes there are some consequences.
But Jesus for these did atone.

There are no excuses for ignorance
God's attributes are clearly seen.
The choice is up to you
Will you rebel or let God redeem?

Just the intricacy of the human body,
The moon and stars set in place,
The sunshine that warms, the air we breathe,
These are all gifts of God's mercy and grace.

May your story be one of triumph
You've overcome by Jesus' blood and your testimony.
Then it will minister to future generations
In spite of this world's baloney.

LIVING WATER

We should be a fountain
Of mercy and forgiveness too.
A wide open vessel
For Jesus' love to flow through.

A flood of graciousness and kindness
Tender and compassionate.
Binding up the wounds of those
Caught in the enemy's net.

A tide of joy and thanksgiving
Our praises should fill the air.
Then the very presence of Jesus
Will certainly be there.

A river of peace and patience
That comforts the weary soul.
The peace that passes understanding
Will wash and make men whole.

A geyser of the Gospel of truth
God's Word will not return void.
It will go forth and accomplish His will
And the results will be enjoyed.

MOLEHILLS & MOUNTAINS

The more you talk about a problem
The larger it will grow.
You explain it over and over
To everyone you know.

Now faith flies out the window
And fear takes its place.
You've made a molehill into a mountain
That is difficult to erase.

Unless you turn back to the Lord
And give the problem to Him.
Your future is in jeopardy
And victory you'll never win.

You must speak positive over the situation
Knowing that God is on your side.
He will be there to fight the battle
But you must decide.

Do you want to keep wallowing in misery
Or stand up and begin to fight?
Your mountains are but ant hills
In the Father's sight.

No matter the outcome,
When you've put your faith into action
Jesus will work it out for your good
And this will bring you satisfaction.

So, refuse to use negative words
For positive words have great power.
Life and death are in the power of the tongue
So, let them be sweet not sour.

MYSTERY

No matter how smart the scholar
There are still new things to discover.
This world is an interesting place
We don't even understand each other.

Since God created the Universe
Men will never understand it all.
When a man thinks he is so smart
He will suddenly hit a brick wall.

For thousands of years men have studied
And great strides they have made.
But there is still so much potential
And a high price has been paid.

Lives lost in exploration
In new experiments and other things.
New discoveries every day
And the satisfaction that this brings.

God planned it all before time began
And He did it for me and you.
We would never give up or be bored
It's exciting to discover something new.

If man in his evil doesn't destroy the world
There will be wonders and marvels ahead.
Future generations will marvel
And our story will be read.

Only as we become Christians
Can we turn this world around,
Change what was evil into good
And declare this, Holy Ground.

NEW DEPTHS

God is always preparing something new
So we don't grow stagnant or stale.
Yet we cling to the familiar
We're afraid that we might fail.

If the plans are from God
Then we need have no fear.
He wants to lead us to new pastures
And messages we need to hear.

New places to go, new people to meet
To share our lives with them.
To reflect the light of His love
And draw them closer to Him.

If we are content to stay where we are
Among old friends, safe and secure.
We miss out on new opportunities
And our choices will become fewer.

If we step out in trust and faith
Knowing God orders our steps.
We'll soar like eagles to new heights
And our faith will reach new depths.

We'll discover that change is fun
New challenges that help us grow.
We look back in appreciation
That God said to us, "Now go!"

OPEN HAND

God's word says in Deuteronomy
To open our hand wide to the poor.
For blessing brings blessings to the giver
And inspires us to even give more.

The poor will always be with us.
To reveal what is in our heart.
Many give without really loving.
But God's love will set us apart.

Self-centeredness is from the devil.
Who would like you to behave like him,
To look down with distain on others.
And show no mercy to then.

A gift, though small, given freely.
Will bless someone in ways we don't see.
But Jesus is quick to take notice.
And says, "It's like giving to Me."

So, don't hesitate when you see a need.
To offer what you have to give.
Then life will take on new meaning.
Joy and peace reign as long as you live.

OUR BODY – HIS TEMPLE

Our body is God's temple
We must treat it with care.
If we've been born again
The Holy Spirit lives in there.

What we eat and what we drink
Is the fuel that we burn.
There is much information out there
We need to study and to learn.

Free sunshine and fresh air
God has provided for us.
So, get out there and move
Don't sit down and rust.

Rest and relaxation are important
Stress takes a terrible toll.
It affects our mind, will, and emotions
For these make up our soul.

Ignorance is no excuse
God holds us each one accountable.
If we will pay attention
Good health is attainable.

Drugs, alcohol, and cigarettes
We know the harm they bring.
When we ask God for help
And desire to get rid of that thing,

We can enjoy better health
Live a life that pleases our Maker,
Bear fruit for His kingdom,
Be a giver, not a taker.

OUR CHILDREN

You are My precious daughter
So, hold your head up high.
I know that you are hurting
And I hear your anxious cry.

You did your very best
With the knowledge that you had.
You took them to Church regularly
With or without their Dad.

You are not responsible
For your child's salvation anymore.
They each are on their own
Like they have never been before.

They must make their own decisions
And pay the consequences as well.
They may walk the narrow way,
Or take the road to hell.

You just pray for them diligently
The Holy Spirit will draw them near.
You prepared them in the past,
Now they must open their ears to hear.

If I promised you beforehand
They would be saved before the end,
The Holy Spirit will work things out.
For on My promise, you can depend.

Each one is responsible for their destiny.
I love and care for each daughter and son.
I know ahead what path they will take,
So, you rest in peace – My beloved one.

OUR FIRE

Just as a physical fire must have wood
So must our spiritual fire.
We must continue to feed it God's word
To keep burning is our heart's desire.

When we have fellowship together
Our flame burns brighter, it's true.
When we pray for and encourage each other
Our passion gains a brighter hue.

More dross will be burned in the fire
Just as iron sharpens iron.
We are moving together as one
To God's beautiful mountain Zion.

Apart our embers grow cold
And our witness is damp and chill.
As we lose our enthusiasm
Then the enemy comes in for the kill.

We must quickly recover our balance
Seek God and pray like never before.
We have come so close to losing it all
That it shakes us to our core.

We determine to stoke the embers
To burn with passion once more.
To worship, study, and fellowship,
And to apathy, we shut the door.

A steady flame is necessary
So, replenish and stoke it each day.
Then we'll be ready to overcome
Whatever may come our way.

OUR LIFESTYLE

The Bible says to avoid all appearance of evil
People are always watching us.
If we claim to be Christians and fall
They look at us in disgust.

We represent Jesus in this life
And we must not let Him down.
We smile in spite of circumstances
While others just wear a frown.

If we behave one way in public
And another way at home.
We need to change this situation
It's something God would not condone.

If we are living with someone not our spouse
Though nothing sexual is taking place.
People will wonder and gossip
As a Christian it brings disgrace.

So, let's live our lives above reproach
Reflect Jesus in all that we do.
Then others will be drawn to Him
And they can be born anew.

REALITY

The talker, the worrier, and the procrastinator.
All talk about something they do not possess
Only God knows the future.
And the things that are best.

The talker thinks he controls the future.
He talks of pie in the sky.
He dreams big things that never happen.
And then he wonders, why?

The worrier sees problems that never come.
But he continually thinks they could.
He always expects trouble.
And never anything good.

The procrastinator never gets around to it.
He puts it off, till another day.
He never accomplishes anything.
Just delay, after delay.

Time is in our Father's hands.
Only He knows what the future will bring.
As we trust and follow His plan for our lives.
He'll bless us with everything.

"Do not boast about tomorrow,
for you know not what a day may bring."
(Proverbs 27:1)

REALLY WORSHIPPING

On the mountain with Elijah
God did not speak through thunder.
But in a still small voice
This should make us stop and wonder.

Do we assume that God is deaf?
Must we be loud to get His attention?
With all the flashing lights
Too numerous to mention.

Must people be stirred into a frenzy
To fill the air with praise?
Is it just because I'm older?
Or is this just a passing craze?

We know that sound above a certain decibel
Causes damage to our ears.
Our young people will be deaf
Before their golden years.

God knows our thoughts before we think them
So, we know He hears our soft voice.
We don't have to yell and scream
In order to rejoice.

We can clap, sing, and even dance
And be filled with excitement and joy.
Now we're really worshipping
And others around, we won't annoy.

THE HOLY SPIRIT AND EARTHWORMS

The Holy Spirit works in the darkness of our hearts
To bring truth to the light.
Earthworms also work in the darkness
Always hidden from our sight.

The Holy Spirit turns into a heart of flesh
One that was made of stone.
The earthworms are always busy underground
Working the soil all alone.

The earthworms eat what we call garbage
They are smart, they don't eat junk.
We could learn a lesson from them
The fast food claims we can debunk.

Worms intuitively know what to do
It's built into their DNA.
Our conscience knows right from wrong
The Holy Spirit pricks us through the day.

The worms wrap around each other with a hug
That's how they show their love.
We are to love others as ourselves
For love is the nature of our Father above.

Just as earthworms work diligently
To turn dry, dead, dirt into black gold,
We must lead people into God's vineyard
And that should be our goal.

So be thankful for the lowly worms
And for the Holy Spirit as well.
Both sent from our loving Father
To make earth a better place to dwell.

THE MEAL THAT HEALS

As we combine Jesus' body and blood with our faith
Healing will take place.
There is no sickness in heaven
No, not even a trace.

Jesus spent one third of His ministry on earth
Healing and delivering the sick.
The enemy comes to kill, steal, and destroy
And his tactics are underhanded and slick.

He uses our imaginations
To make things worse than they are.
Then he bombards us with new symptoms
Many of them are bizarre.

It's our responsibility to care of our temple
With the proper food, exercise, and rest.
To pray and obey God's directions
And to avoid life's strain and stress.

Many sicknesses have spiritual roots
That we need to seek and find.
So, we can deal with the root
And gain understanding in our mind.

Every perfect gift comes from our Father
Who wants us healed and whole.
We must learn to stand in authority
To break the enemy's hold.

Now we can walk in victory
Because Jesus has paid the cost.
We are more than conquerors
And the enemy he has lost.

THE NARROW ROAD

In his poem, Robert Frost wrote:
"Two roads diverged in a yellow wood ...
I took the one less traveled by,
And that has made all the difference"
In the things that caught my eye.

God's Word tells us the broad way
That is traveled by many leads to destruction.
But we chose the narrow one that leads to life
For we have listened to God's instruction.

We face many choices in life
And we encounter the consequences they bring.
The good ones inspired by the Spirit
They will cause our heart to sing.

The bad choices bring consequences
We may not like to face.
But once that action is taken
The results we cannot erase.

The world beckons us to follow the crowd
There is excitement and pleasure there.
We can think and do whatever we please
But this is the devil's snare.

As we follow Jesus instead of others
We will arrive at the right place.
Our journey will be successful
And of regret, there won't be a trace.

TOLERANCE

Tolerance is a tool of fools
They use it to deceive even the elect.
It makes us question our beliefs
And if we let it, make our life a wreck.

Liberals use it all the time
To make God's children feel ashamed.
The liberal media plays it up
And for hate crimes we are blamed.

The enemy's tactics are always underhanded
He uses people to do his dirty work.
Yet our liberties are at stake
While the liberals sit back and smirk.

As long as we follow God's commandments
And treat others as we would be treated.
We know that truth and love will win
And the enemy will be defeated.

WELCOME HIM

The Holy Spirit can be received, resisted, or rejected
This decision is ours alone.
We can't both be in control
Only one is seated on the throne.

We can do it our own way
We think that we know best.
We may even rise to the top
Others thinking that we're a great success.

But inside, we are empty
Of the things that make life blessed.
We must keep on climbing that ladder
While inside we are stressed.

There is no peace or joy
For worldly things will never satisfy.
Satan will tell us different
But we know that he's a lie.

These are the gifts of the Holy Spirit
That only He can give.
We must welcome Him into our hearts
If a meaningful life we want to live.

WINDOWS

If my eyes are the windows of my soul
Look and what do you see?
Do you see Jesus down there?
Or do you see a reflection of me?

Do I really trust everything to Jesus
Is He the one in control?
Or is it all just pretense?
I'm playing the Christian role.

I may fool others, but I can't fool God
For He sees what's in my heart.
He knows if I love and serve Him
Or if I'm still just playing a part.

It's time I get serious with God
To be sure my motives are pure,
That Jesus is seated on the throne of my life,
Then my future is safe and secure.

WINTER

The trees are undressing
It's time for winter to begin.
We should examine our life
Drop off any burden or sin.

It's a time to grow deep roots
Quiet our souls –rest in peace.
Slow this rapid race called life
Let Christ grow in us, as we decrease.

A season to look back and see
Have we moved forward or backward this year?
Has our trust and faith in God grown stronger?
Have we given others a listening ear?

As the trees stand bare in winter
So are we in God's light.
He sees the motives in our heart
These are hidden from man's sight.

Is He pleased or is He sad?
That's a question we should ask.
Have we procrastinated or simply forgotten?
Will the things we've accomplished last?

Have we led some soul to Jesus?
Or helped someone else to grow.
These are the things that effect eternity
And set our hearts aglow.

So, let's examine our motives
Are they selfish or sincere?
We'll stand before the judgment seat
With peace or with fear.

WORDS

Words can alter an atmosphere
Words can change a life.
Words can cause separation
Between a husband and his wife.

Words can cause a war
Or still the angry sea.
Words are powerful weapons
On this we can agree.

So why aren't we careful with our words?
We often speak before we think.
Yet words can spark a fire of fury
Quicker than a wink.

Offence is caused by what we say
And it drives others far away.
But our kind and loving words
Make people want to stay.

With gossip, words discredit people
Yet, God sees it as a sin.
It's usually spoken behind one's back
So, their good name, they can't defend.

Over and over again in His Word
God tells us to be slow to speak.
He looks down on the arrogant know–it–all
But He honors the lowly and meek.

Someday, we have to give account
Of all the words we say.
We'll really get ahead in life
If we're slow to speak, and swift to obey.

WRONG THINKING

There are many things we think are in the Bible
That simply are not there.
We use them in our daily talk
When we have something we want to share.

God says that we perish for lack of knowledge
We hate to admit it, but this is true.
How well do you know God's word?
Is it easy to confuse you?

We say things without even thinking
We have heard them quoted so long.
So, we take for granted that they are true
And often they are totally wrong.

The simple solution to this dilemma
We need to know the Word better.
We're told not to take away or add to the Word.
Not a jot, a tittle or a letter.

I AM
SPEAKING

To My Children

OUR GIFTS

A GEM

All snowflakes come from the same source,
Yet not one of them is alike.
As God made each one of us different,
We are each His special delight.

He gives gifts and talents
And they are equal in His sight.
They will bring Him glory
When we learn to handle them right.

It's when jealousy rears its ugly head,
And we envy another's gift,
The enemy comes in to stir up trouble,
And causes among us a rift.

Don't compare yourself to others
They are not your concern.
They each belong to God
And comparison tends to bring ruin.

We each must cherish the gift we're given,
Do our utmost to fulfill our role.
This should lift Jesus higher
And that should be our goal.

It may be menial: like cleaning the church,
But when we do it as unto Him.
In Heaven, it won't be wood, hay or stubble,
Instead it will be a gem!

A PROPHET

The Bible tells us when you bless a prophet,
A prophet's reward you will receive.
So, the opposite must be true
When you set out to hurt or deceive.

God does not take this lightly
For His prophets are close to His heart.
Your hedge of protection will come down.
His mercy and grace will depart.

A prophet's life isn't an easy one,
Consider God's prophet Moses.
The Israelites complained and rebelled.
His life was never a bed of roses.

God gives them a hard assignment
Warnings the people don't want to hear
It's always for their protection,
And to bring God's presence near.

So always show respect for His prophet
Bless and pray for them too.
Then you will receive a prophet's reward.
And their blessings will rest on you.

ANGELS IN WAITING MINISTRY TEAM

Maybe we lived a few days or weeks
Or we died in our mother's womb.
We went straight to the arms of Jesus
We are not in that lonely tomb.

Thanks to you ladies who cared enough
You fashioned a garment from a wedding dress.
We were enfolded in beauty
Before our bodies were laid to rest.

Now we are growing and rejoicing in Heaven
We're with all of the other children there.
We just want to say thanks
To those women who showed they care.

You blessed our parents as well
By the love that you showed to them.
Your reward will be in Heaven
For you do it as unto Him.

FAITH AS A MUSTARD SEED

There is potential power wrapped up in us
Just as in the mustard seed,
To become a mighty warrior for Jesus
And to help all those in need.

God gives us a measure of faith
Then it's up to us to make it grow.
We must feed on God's Word, then be obedient
We'll grow stronger each time we face our foe.

We know how to speak to our mountain
And command it to move.
Then whatever was standing in our way
Will disappear – the way is smooth.

People can then come to us
We'll be shelter in life's storm.
We have words of comfort and reconciliation
We will be wise, above the norm.

God knows He can depend on us
We're His ambassadors on this earth.
We have stood through many battles
And proven to Him, our worth.

FOLLOW THE FRUIT

We should chase the Fruit of the Spirit, not the gifts
If we want to be effective in our ministry.
To serve, a vessel must be clean and pure
That's simple, elemental chemistry.

Without *love* and *goodness*, we've nothing to give
To a sick and dying world.
The Fruit of the Spirit is precious
In God's eyes it's like a beautiful pearl.

When we act without *patience*
We jump ahead of God's plan.
Then when things go awry
We don't even understand.

Our *joy* is what draws others
For they want what they see in us.
Then *peace* enters in the mixture
We don't quarrel and fuss.

God is gentle and longsuffering with us
So, we should exhibit this trait.
We keep ministering in spite of setbacks
Hoping we're not too late.

To rescue someone from Satan's snare
Who has misled and lied to them.
But as we are *faithful* in our ministry
We will snatch them away from him.

Last, but not least
If we want to reach our goal—
This one is the hardest to attain
And it's called *self-control.*

It's fruit that we are to bear
For it feeds the hungry soul.
Without it what we offer is empty
And will never make a man whole.

OUR GIFTS

When we are bearing much fruit
The gifts will follow as the Holy Spirit wills.
We'll see miracles and wonders again
And we'll follow along for the thrills.

FULFILLED

Food draws more eaters than prayer draws seekers
This is such a sad situation.
We are fat physically and starved spiritually
And that is no exaggeration.

Praise and worship and prayer combined
Form a powerful wall of protection.
Yet people neglect these important things
And withhold their tithe in rejection.

God is the giver of all good gifts
Yet we withhold so much from Him.
We reason that we may need it ourselves
No wonder our spiritual light is so dim.

If we could only realize if we give and love
They become a flowing stream
That nourishes others as well as us
And fulfills our every dream.

Go

The more we grow in our relationship with God
The more we will mirror His care for those in need.
He has promised in His Word
To give to the sower His seed.

These are the words in the Bible
That we share to help others grow.
This is why we can't stand still.
God always tells us to go

Into the highways and byways
Wherever we find we've been sent.
Evil has been here since time began
It is by no means a current event.

We overcome evil only with love
As we minister to others in need.
Then, God will be there to help us
As the poor and needy, we feed.

We are God's ambassadors in this world
What kind of example do others see?
Do we sacrifice and go out of our way
To see the captives set free?

Or are we content to stay in our comfort zone
Thinking others will fulfill the call?
We need to wake up and take inventory
Or we could be the one to fall.

God did not put us here to occupy space
But we are poured-out wine and broken bread.
Get up and move and be involved
Lest your life end, and you are dead.

Handle With Care

Don't say I'll prophesy or give a word
The gifts are the Spirit's, who gives as He wills.
They should bring honor to the Father
It is His desire that it always fulfills.

The gifts should edify and build up the body
One can never say: "They are mine."
For then they glorify that person.
That is never God's design.

Newly baptized people can be easily led astray
If they are not grounded in God's Word.
Then, they will not recognize the control
They will simply follow the herd.

They need our prayers more than ever
God has put them in our care.
The enemy tries to sneak in a new way
We must guard them from his snare.

All the gifts must be handled with care
Or the enemy can cause much destruction.
So be wise as a serpent – gentle as a dove
And things will smoothly function.

LIGHT

Father help me to not think less of myself
But to think of myself less.
I should be pouring out to others
And not worry about the rest.

Let's use the gifting God has bestowed on us
As it's poured out; it sets others on fire.
They are inspired to seek their gifting
This should be our underlying desire.

We are not to hide our light under a bushel
But put it on a hill to give light.
To draw others to Jesus
He's the one who restores their sight.

Together our light disperses the darkness
This is where the enemy tries to hide.
His deeds are exposed in the light
And people realize how he lied.

Now, their eyes are opened to the truth
That Jesus is the Life and the Way.
The Light of the world to all men
Now, their night has been turned to day.

NEW ANOINTING

God won't give you a new anointing
Unless there is a new vessel to put it in.
God is never wasteful
Nor will He tolerate sin.

Our vessel must be pure and holy
Through which God's words can flow.
Our motives never self-centered
Nor emotions that come and go.

When we stand strong in our beliefs
And know that God's Word is true.
Then, He sends dreams, words, and visions
And He can use even you.

When we put God and His Word first
Above all earthly fame.
His Word will flow through us
And bring glory to His name.

OUR DESTINY

Before we can move in a higher calling
In life we must walk it out.
The call must be so clear to us
That we never tend to doubt.

The walk may not be easy and pleasant
But it is the only way.
Many don't want to pay the price
There are others who will simply delay.

A higher calling will bring such joy
That we wonder why we hesitated.
We could have been there years ago
Now it's come, but it is belated.

Maybe we were not spiritually ready
So, the time was not right
We have to grow in maturity
So we can win the fight.

Now, the time has finally come
God moves in us in a powerful way.
He gives us words that change lives
Just by the words that we say.

We are making a difference in people
And we are fulfilling our destiny.
What a wonderful privilege it is
To become who God designed us to be.

OUR GIFTS

When God gives gifts to His children
He does not take them back.
They are to be used to build His kingdom
This is a Biblical fact.

It is a dangerous thing
When we use them to build up self.
To impress other people
Or to gain fame or material wealth.

We must not envy other's gifts
God gives us each our own.
Each one is special when we use it wisely
God did not make us a clone.

So diligently seek your own gifting
Then use it with caution and fear.
God will bless you in many ways
And draw you ever near.

God will not share His glory with anyone
So, let's be careful with the gift He's given.
It's meant to benefit others and glorify Him
And our reward will be in Heaven.

OUR YOUTH

The vibrancy of youth
Brings excitement to the air.
The energy that they display
Makes us happy to be there.

To see so many young people
Hearts set on fire.
The plans of the enemy
Are indeed looking dire.

God is preparing an army
To lead us in this battle.
We must prepare ourselves to follow
Let these old bones rattle.

The outcome will be glorious
Better than the eclipse.
We will all see God's glory
When the balance of power flips.

God is using our youth
To accomplish a new thing.
What a joy to be a part of this
God's end time awakening

OUR GIFTS

PATIENCE

We learn to practice patience
In the fiery furnace of affliction.
It is here that God comes close
And pronounces His benediction.

We recognize our trials as God's winepress
So, there will flow from us refreshing truth.
That Jesus came to redeem us
And we are His living proof.

Patience is a powerful force
That people will recognize.
It puts us with intolerable situations
We love people who others despise.

Patience just keeps on keeping on
Month after month, year after year.
When God sees this fruit in our life
It draws His presence near.

We are so thankful for God's patience
We wonder how He puts up with us.
So many times, we mess up and fail
It's a wonder He doesn't give up in disgust.

We will never comprehend God's great love
It looks beyond our faults and shame.
He remembers He formed and breathed life in us
And we, His children, bear His name.

Do we care enough to keep praying for people
Or do we give up in despair?
God didn't give up on us
So, let's determine to do our share.

We will find that patience brings joy in our life
We look forward to each challenge God brings
As we overcome each obstacle
Then our spirit will take wings.

PEACE

Seek peace at any cost
For in it our souls will find rest.
The things that entangle us in life
Will be exchanged for those God thinks best.

He knows the things we really need
Usually different than what we think.
Some things hold us back from our potential
And peace may be the missing link.

When we have peace about a situation
We can move forward with confidence.
The road may have bumps and turns
But success will be our recompense.

Peace will always pave the way
It takes no extra effort on our part.
People will want what we have
The peace that flows from God's heart.

Peace will calm a storm
It will heal a troubled soul.
It will guard us in times of tribulation
So, let's make peace our final goal.

POURED OUT

You can never set aside for God
Something you desire for yourself.
It is not worthy of Him if it cost you nothing
Be it blessings, money, or health.

When I realize that something is too wonderful for me
Then, I pour it out to God instead.
Then, He will pour out rivers of water through me
So others will be watered and fed.

If we become bitter and sour
It's when we hoarded a blessing that God gave to us.
People will never see God in our lives
And we have forfeited His trust.

Even spiritual blessing must be poured out
Though common sense says it's absurd.
It's hard to sacrifice the things we cherish
Yet, God demands it in His Word.

We must guard against lusting after spiritual things
We just seek God in everything we do.
Then blessings will naturally flow through us
Be as refreshing as the morning dew.

THE ATMOSPHERE

There are so many things that we can do
To change the atmosphere.
It can be bright and sunny
Or it can be dark and filled with fear.

When we walk into the room
Do we wear a smile or do we frown?
People will be lifted up
Or we can pull them down.

Just by our joy and laughter
We can brighten a dreary day.
People's burdens will be lifted
By the interest that we display.

Forgiveness frees the perpetrator
And it frees us as well.
It brings great joy in Heaven
And it shakes the gates of hell.

So, let's always be upbeat and positive
No matter the circumstances.
This will lift all of our spirits
And our atmosphere it enhances.

Unique

Every person is unique in God's sight
He does not make junk.
Don't let words pull you down
They are just a lot of bunk.

Some people are full of jealousy
When they see others succeed.
There is a void inside of them
And it's Jesus that they need.

God has given us all gifts and talents
You must discern the one that fits you.
It involves going into action
And not just sitting in a pew.

Maybe it's just being a friend
Or lending someone a listening ear.
Whatever brings people closer to Jesus
And helps their muddled thoughts to clear.

As long as we don't try to do it on our own
And we let God work through us.
It will make this world a better place
And fill the enemy with disgust.

WORSHIP

A true heart of worship
Is the best fire insurance we possess.
With it we keep the enemy at bay.
And render him powerless.

When worship flows from our heart
It pleases the heart of our Father.
Then we realize that we have blessed Him
And it makes us try even harder.

As we raise our praise together
It opens Heaven's doors.
Now God's blessings are not hindered
And out of His throne, it pours.

Now we're covered with blessing and favor
And our life will be full to the brim.
So, drop off all inhibitions
And pour out your worship to Him.

I AM
SPEAKING

TO MY CHILDREN

PRAYERS

DAILY PRAYER

Jesus, without You as the Light of the world
We would have nothing to look forward to at all.
Chaos would reign all over the earth
No hope for man since the fall.

This must be what hell would be like
Darkness and death all around.
The absence of love and compassion
Moans of agony, the only sound.

O Lord, open men's eyes to the truth
That they must turn to Jesus and live.
Now is the time to repent
Before it's too late to forgive.

Show men what hell would be like
So, no one would want to go there.
I fall on my knees and intercede
This is my daily prayer.

EXPECTATION

Never limit God's unlimited power
By our limited expectations.
He has been performing miracles
In all previous generations.

From the days when Jesus walked on earth
To this very present hour.
We've seen miracles and wonders
They demonstrate His power.

So why do we put God in a box
Expecting nothing when we pray.
Faith is always believing
In the words that we say.

God created everything with words
Words have power when backed by faith.
So, don't be double minded
Just boldly knock on Heaven's gate.

Believe that God is who He says He is
And can do what He does promise.
Stand strong just like Abraham
Don't be a doubting Thomas.

Then, wait patiently for God's answer
It will always be the right one.
He knows our needs before we ask
For He loves each daughter and son.

HEALING

Lord, if you could use a donkey
Then I know You can use me.
I believe You are my healer
And desire to set men free.

I want to see people's tumors fall off
And all cancers disappear.
To see blind eyes opened
Deaf ears once more to hear.

Jesus used miracles and healings
To draw men unto Him.
What is wrong with me, Lord?
Is Your presence in me so slim?

I believe with all of my heart
I just need to see it manifested.
People need Your healing touch
Is my faith just being tested?

Holy Spirit give me the gift of faith
So, I can do God's will.
I'm waiting patiently on You
My heart's desire, please fulfill.

It breaks my heart to see Your children
Suffering untold misery.
I just want someone to come, to heal
Even if it can't be me.

Make A Difference

Lord, I am so honored
Just to be Your child.
Each day I try to do something
That I know will make You smile.

Your heart must be burdened
With all the iniquity on earth.
The depravity of man
Life counted as no worth.

Your children are precious to You, Lord
Yet, they are crushed and abused.
Put in cages like animals
Many are falsely accused.

Yet, you have patience with all of us
Waiting for us to see the light.
To rise up as that mighty army
That can put the enemy to flight.

We can make a difference
If we win just one soul.
They can reach out to others
And many will be made whole.

Salvation for your children
Is your heart's desire.
In brokenness I cry out Lord
Please set my heart on fire.

OUR CRY

Jesus, You are the beginning and the end
And You are everything in between.
You are ruler over all we see
And those that are unseen.

You look into our hearts
And see our every desire.
You can take the hardest heart
And set it afire.

Nothing is impossible with You
The world rests in Your hands.
Your children cry out for mercy
Angels stand ready for Your commands.

Evil has triumphed over good
The earth cries out in agony.
We have failed so miserably in our task
To guard and tend this earth for Thee.

Now judgment stands at the door
We deserve it – that is true.
Yet we cry out once more for mercy
We can only depend on You.

Will you intervene this time?
Or will persecution be in store?
Maybe then we will fall on our knees
Repent and pray like never before.

Our Prayers

The Holy Spirit takes our feeble prayers
And turns them into something great.
They go straight to the throne of God
And results they then create.

When we pray in the spirit
It is so power-filled.
That the enemy is overwhelmed
And his venom is distilled.

God hears our every prayer
And the answer is on its way.
As we wait in confidence
It will not delay.

If it involves another person's will
The time may not be right.
But God is true to His promises
Though they are hidden from our sight.

Don't grow weary in waiting
Things will turn out right in the end.
The Holy Spirit is working in their lives
And the answer lies around the bend.

Our patience and persistence
Help us to grow strong.
We've passed the test of time
And we know to God, we belong.

OUR START

Just five minutes spent with God and His Word
Is worth more than all the rest of our day.
Many have such busy schedules
But even the busiest of us can pray.

On our drive to work, or on the bus
Pause and turn your thoughts toward Heaven.
God is always there to listen
He knows the time we've been given.

Don't neglect to put on your armor
Our spirits need this in place.
The enemy is ever watchful
And the rest of our day may be a race.

When we're so busy, we're not as aware
Of the traps that Satan has laid.
He wants to take our attention from God
So our spiritual progress will be delayed.

But if we've put our armor on
And started our day with prayer,
The roadblocks the enemy puts in our way
Will be exposed and laid bare.

Then we will avoid much heartache
Grow deeper in our trust.
It's all because we started with God
So, we see why that's a must.

PASSING THROUGH

I'd rather be known in Heaven, feared in
Hell, than recognized on earth.
I've belonged to you Lord,
Since the day of my new birth.

My name is written in your Book of Life
On earth, I'm just passing through.
When I've accomplished my mission here
I'll be ready to come home to you.

The perils and snares are all around.
But You give me strength to resist.
Joy and peace surround me
I'm immersed in their midst.

I pray I leave this earth a better place
Because of the time I spent here.
The souls I've won or just encouraged
These things I will ever hold dear.

Pray

The prayer of the feeblest Saint
Strikes terror in the heart of Satan.
Why do so many hesitate to pray
Do they think his fury they'll awaken?

No! Jesus has defeated him
Is this the one who makes the nations tremble?
If we compare him to our God
There's nothing in him to even resemble

The glorious splendor of our God
Who is awesome in power and might.
He is the One who created Satan
Who was perfect in His sight.

Then pride came in and he changed
He wanted to take God's place.
So, he was cast out of Heaven
And forfeited God's mercy and grace.

Now, he seeks to destroy God's children
In underhanded and devious ways.
But we need not fear his tactics
For he flees when a Christian prays.

PRIVILEGE

Prayer is an awesome privilege
To converse with the God of the universe.
He understands when we don't have the words
It's from our heart, we don't have to rehearse.

God is touched with our infirmity
He has known us from the womb.
He desires the very best from us
And delights to see us bloom.

To bear fruit for His kingdom
Brings pleasure beyond compare.
He blesses and anoints us
So His love and gifts we can share.

Prayer paves the way for miracles
That this unbelieving world needs to see.
The Holy Spirit is the power
But it flows through you and me.

Prayer and fasting go hand in hand
To make us a channel to flow through.
Then God can use us in a mighty way
To bear witness to the things that are true.

Are you willing to take the time
To pour out your life, if need be,
To bring the kingdom of Heaven to earth,
So all men, His glory, will see.

QUIET TIME

Lord, You come in the quietness
Like a soft and gentle breeze.
If we are truly listening
We will fall on our knees

In worship and homage to You, Lord
That You would speak to us.
The Master of the Universe
And we are but dust.

Your care for us is beyond description
For You love us in spite of our sin.
You see us through the blood of Jesus
It's on Him that we depend.

You are not disturbed by our imperfections
Nor are You impressed by our piety.
We can't hide behind a mask
Like we can from society.

You know our thoughts before we think them
And You long to call us Your own.
As we yield ourselves completely to You
In our lives You're seated on the throne.

We must spend quiet time alone with You
To receive all You have to give.
Life will be filled with new opportunities
Because now we've begun to truly live.

The Father's Heart

When you give prayer top priority
I will move Heaven and earth to answer your call.
So humble yourselves, listen to My voice
And I will explain it all.

I have told you in My Word
To always seek My Kingdom first.
You don't understand when your efforts seem futile
And My children are dying of thirst.

You have put business in front of prayer
Then wonder why miracles are not taking place.
When you get on your knees and pray
I will reveal My Face.

When you finally see Me in My Glory
You will speak, and mountains will move.
I know the plans I have for you
But your loyalty you must prove.

Then all things on earth will be shaken
People everywhere will fall on their knees.
Revivals will break out all over the place
When My heart, with prayers, you please.

When you really expect great things
Then great things, you will see.
Know that I look on your heart
And your prayers are pleasing to Me.

THE MAIN THING

Prayer is the main thing
When we talk to our Creator.
We need to do it now
Don't put it off till later.

God's ear is always attentive
To His children's voices below.
He is waiting to hear from us
About the things we want to know.

He loves to hear us thank Him
For all the things He's done.
Too many times we hurl requests
For we are always on the run.

What really pleases Him the most
Is when we clear off our agenda.
When we spend time in His presence
With nothing allowed to hinder

Our sweet fellowship with Jesus.
They are the Three in One.
Releasing all our burdens
They seemed to weigh a ton.

Now we are free to accomplish so much
More than we would have before.
For we will find at the Master's feet
Pleasures forevermore.

THOUGHTS

God knows our thoughts before we think them
But thoughts are not always prayers.
Maybe our eyes have been blinded
And this is another of the enemy's snares.

A thought can be spoken aloud
Proclaimed into the atmosphere.
Then it will bring about change
For both God and Satan will hear.

It brings joy to our Father's heart
But fear to the enemy's ear.
Now the situation will change
Signs and wonders may appear.

When we pray God's Word aloud
It has power like a hurricane.
God will move into action
For we have invoked Jesus' precious name.

God always honors His Son
He was the fulfillment of His Word on earth.
When our thoughts become vocal
They will bring about new birth.

The birth of another person
Or the birth of an idea or plan.
Now God will move on our behalf
All we have to do is stand.

Then as we wait in anticipation
The answer will be loud and clear.
We can move ahead with confidence
For Heaven has been brought near.

The Word says to speak, not think, to the mountain
And it will be cast into the sea.
So, this prayer must be vocal
For it to become real to me.

WORTH

Lord, I know that I am nothing
What I do doesn't amount to a hill of beans.
It is what You do through me
That saves and redeems.

Unless a grain of wheat is buried
It remains a single thing.
But when it is planted and matures
A bountiful harvest it will bring.

When I die completely to myself
Then Your Spirit is free to flow
Into the lives of others
And then they will know

The fulfillment that comes from surrender
Not needing to do my own thing.
I'll make a difference in my world
For fruitfulness You will bring.

Light will replace darkness
Hope will nudge out fear.
New confidence will flow in,
For I feel Your presence near.

This world will be a better place
For I have lived on earth.
I've given my life to Jesus
And exhibited His matchless worth.

I AM
SPEAKING

To My Children

WITNESSING

FOLLOWING JESUS

When we are walking close to Jesus
We never know how it will be.
We may be spiritually in the desert
Or cheerfully sailing upon the sea.

Sometimes, we are on the mountaintop
Sometimes in the valley below.
We just follow where he leads
And go where he wants us to go.

Sometimes, it's like a roller coaster
With high and then deep emotion.
Where we will be at any given time
We haven't the slightest notion.

We know that it will be fulfilling
For Jesus is in control.
So, we just go with the flow
Now, we are really on a roll.

Lives will be changed – strongholds broken
Things like we've never seen before.
It will always be an adventure
What Jesus has in store.

We'll always make new friends
Who will be with us forever.
Who would be foolish enough
To refuse this enticing endeavor?

God's Grace With Me

Lord, you are with me in the sunshine.
You are with me in the rain.
You are there when I'm happy.
And even closer when I'm in pain.

There is nowhere that I go.
That your presence is not there.
I feel your arms around me.
In comfort and in care.

How I love You, Lord.
You're the reason for my living.
You send me out to comfort others.
By sharing and forgiving.

Now, life is filled with purpose.
To make this world a better place.
To bring others near to you.
That they may share your grace.

GOOD – EVIL

If Satan can take good and turn it into evil
Surely God can take evil and turn it into good.
Satan brings chaos and disunity
God promotes brotherhood.

Like the lyrics to the songs we sing
They can be evil and suggestive.
Leading to death or sexual sin
Many people harassed or molested.

The dance can be beautiful, honoring God
Or it can be filled with sexy gyrations.
Older people are shocked and perplexed
At so many of this younger generation.

Many of our holidays have pagan roots
But God uses them to glorify his name.
The birth of his Son, his resurrection
So, don't view them with distain.

Some only go to Church on Christmas and Easter
And they hear the gospel spoken.
Seeds are planted that may grow and blossom
And the enemy's hold has been broken.

Holidays touch the hardest heart
And when hearts are softened, souls are won.
No matter where the origin started
God's will has now been done.

GOOD PEOPLE

It's not the good people who go to Heaven
But those who have been redeemed.
It's not necessarily those with wealth, or education
That by Heaven's standards are highly esteemed.

It's the humble and lowly in heart
Who are servants to others around,
Not the haughty and demanding
Who will be standing on Holy Ground.

Jesus, though the Son of God
Made Himself a servant to all.
We must die to self daily
In order to answer His call.

The thief on the cross is a good example
He knew he had sinned and deserved to die.
When he accepted Jesus as Lord
He went to reign with Him on high.

Only the blood of Jesus
Can atone for our sin.
When we walk with Him daily
He will cleanse us from within.

Then we are assured of salvation
His peace reigns in our heart.
Now, life is worth living
We're sanctified and set apart.

HIGHWAY

This road I am traveling is the highway to Heaven
There will be many stops along the way.
I know that Jesus walks with me
New scenery and adventures every day.

There may be trouble and danger ahead
But I will not fear or fret.
I know that my Father has planned it all
And my destination is a sure bet.

May the fruit of the Spirit be evident in me
So others may taste and know
That Jesus is everything they need
So they flourish and begin to grow.

I will make detours along the way
Some will be good, some a mistake.
Others will be watching to see how I do
Then, they may decide to follow in my wake.

So, I must pray and fast to stay strong.
To follow closely God's will for me.
So I can lead them to the cross of Christ.
For there, they will be set free.

Then, their journey on this highway begins
They will have adventures of every kind.
But they are on the right road
And they won't be left behind.

HIS SONG

I'm a nut for Jesus.
I don't care what people think of me.
I sing, clap, shout, and jump around.
For he has set me free.

Others do this at ballgames.
In honor of mortal men.
I do it for Jesus.
He's my savior and my friend.

He deserves all of my praises.
He died so I might live.
So, I'll praise Him with my every breath.
With all my love I freely give.

Many are just drunk with alcohol.
I'm filled with his new wine.
If they could just taste of Jesus?
Then their lives would be like mine.

He said, "If anyone is thirsty.
Come take a drink from Me."
When they take a drink of his love
Their eyes will be open to see.

Life has taken on new meaning.
Joy, that flows forth in praise.
Now they are a nut for Jesus.
And they worship in crazy ways.

I am the older generation.
So, they think I'm befuddled in my head.
While they stand there like a stone
I think to myself: they must be dead.

If we can't shout and celebrate Jesus?
There is something seriously wrong.
He gives us life and breath.
And we should be – **His song**.

Horizontal Help

God often sends vertical help
Through horizontal means
He sends what we need through others
He uses the redeemed.

What a privilege to be used by God
He has done so much for us.
But we must be ready to take action
We can't sit around and rust.

There are so many out there in need
God loves and cares for them all.
When we are tuned in to His voice
We will hear and answer His call.

Don't let the right hand know
What the left hand has done.
God will reward us in secret
For over pride, humility has won.

INFLUENCE

If we have people in our Church who are far from God
We are not doing our job.
We have opened the door to the enemy's influence
And let Satan come in to kill and to rob.

The negative influences from the world
If we let them, will smother God's Word.
So, we must guard our heart with all diligence
And discern the things that we've heard.

Are they uplifting and filled with life?
Or do they pull us down?
Jesus gives us life abundantly
He desires to see us smile not frown.

The Jezebel spirit is bent on control
Her friends are like puppets on a string.
Her influence is so strong
That destruction it can bring.

We must hold tight to the truth of God's Word
Don't let other's opinions influence you.
The Holy Spirit is our counselor
He will show what's false or true.

We are ambassadors for Christ
He has entrusted His influence to us.
Are we drawing others to Jesus?
Or has He misplaced His trust?

Our influence is our true treasure
So always handle it with care.
It is a precious gift passed on to others
So only God's truth should we share.

JOY & LAUGHTER

A merry heart doeth good like a medicine
But a broken spirit drieth up the bones.
Why do you think I put these in My word?
My children should be sunbeams not dead stones.

Sunbeams shine and sparkle
They brighten up a room.
They bring in joy and laughter
And chase out fear and gloom.

I dance over you with singing
I want you to reflect My light.
The enemy hides in the darkness
Your laughter brings Me delight.

Study and meditation have their place
But joy comes in the morning.
Clouds and rain will come on earth
They part with a new day dawning.

True happiness and joy act like a magnet
They draw people out of the enemy's trap.
Then we can have a true celebration
We will all rejoice and clap.

We have overcome the enemy
The victory has been won.
We didn't even know it was a chore
We were having so much fun.

LABOR

Why do we labor in vain?
With labor we are supposed to give birth.
God has planted a seed in us.
That has infinite worth.

Jesus labored and His Church was birthed.
And we are the ones who are blessed.
Now he has given the task to us.
We don't want to fail the test.

There are many things to be birthed.
New believers are the first priority.
There are many other things to be fulfilled.
There is a great variety.

Messages to be preached – help to be given.
Maybe just to share your story.
Songs to be sung – work to be done.
As long as it brings God the glory.

We've fulfilled the destiny God planned for us.
As steadfast we remain.
This puts a smile on God's face
That we did not labor in vain.

Lights

Spirit-filled believers are the lights.
Who are reflecting Jesus on earth today.
And we are the only ones.
Who can lead unbelievers in the way.

The way that leads them to the cross
Where salvation can take place.
Night is coming soon.
So, this is the final race.

We must witness like never before.
Precious souls are lost every day.
We can't afford to be timid.
Now is the time – don't delay.

The devil is working overtime.
He knows his time is short.
He is using every trick he knows
For this, his final resort.

We must learn to abort his tactics.
To free those who have ears to hear.
We can snatch them out of the fires of hell.
So, let's act – our call is clear.

Look Again

Look again into God's word
You missed something the first time around.
You have to look really deep
For that's where true riches are found.

Too many times we skim over the words
And don't see what they truly mean.
So, take time to look again
Things might not be what they seem.

A treasure is not always visible
For all of the world to see.
Many of Gods blessings come easily
But some are deep and not free.

We may have to dig and dig
For some are buried deep.
But the joy in finding true treasure
Is something we may want to keep.

And God would have us to share
With others so they may grow.
Then, they may start to look again
To seek and then to know.

LOST SOULS

When was the last time I lay awake and wept for a lost soul?
I would have to answer, "Never."
I have been busy with other things
Probably some other empty endeavor.

Don't let my heart become hardened
To be unmoved and even cynical.
Soften my heart, Lord
May I take self off its pinnacle.

Call me out into the deep
Give me a burden for each lost soul.
Send me into the highways and byways
Quench my fear, make me bold.

Lord, what You reveal you redirect
Down the pathway You have chosen.
May I follow as You lead me
To help thaw those who are frozen.

They've been hurt or turned off by Christians
Often by our superior attitude.
Jesus loved all of God's children
No one would He ever exclude.

So, I will humble myself now
Show others that I really care.
Pray and work like never before
For I have known what it's like to be there.

Someone prayed and reached out to me
Can't You count on me to do the same?
I am equipped by Your Holy Spirit
And I do it all in Jesus' Name.

OIL

Because we are covered in oil
Nothing from the world sticks.
Whether it comes from reprobate men
Or it's just another of the devil's tricks.

Evil thoughts and ideas may come
But they quickly slide away.
Criticism and ridicule
They just fly by, they can't stay.

Be continually under the anointing
This covers us with God's oil.
The things He asks us to do
Are so easy, they never seem like toil.

God anoints us with the oil of gladness
This fills our very sphere.
Just our joy and laughter
Always draw His Spirit near.

When the Holy Spirit comes on the scene
Things begin to explode.
We've been mining in the Word
And we hit the Mother Lode.

God will anoint us with new oil
Then we will shine like His Son.
Just our presence will draw others
And another soul will be won.

ORPHAN GENERATION

There is an orphan generation in our world
They are suffering from abuse or neglect.
Deep down inside often hidden
They feel that they are a reject.

They react in two different ways
They are withdrawn in a shell or in open rebellion.
People don't understand the hurt inside
Instead they are regarded as a hellion.

Many come from one-parent homes
Other parents are too busy for them.
They are left to fend for themselves
And even their future looks dim.

They feel that they are unworthy
They will never be good enough.
They are usually weak and vulnerable
Or they are outwardly calloused and tough.

They have not been told about Jesus and God
That their love doesn't have to be earned
They love us all unconditionally
But that's something they've never learned

We need to tell them our story
That God loves and accepts them each one.
If they surrender their lives to Jesus
They'll become a daughter or son.

No longer alone but part of the family
Loved and nurtured by us as well.
We are brothers and sisters in Christ
And we've saved another one from hell.

OUR HELPER

The Holy Spirit is our link to the Father
To His wisdom, mercy, and love.
Jesus has finished His work on earth
And is now seated in Heaven above.

The Holy Spirit is here to teach and guide us
In the path that God has ordained.
He is the one who prods us onward
When by life's problems we are detained.

He is always gentle and kind
As He seeks to guide us higher.
Satan is always trying to stop us
But we know that he's a liar.

As we learn to listen to that still small voice
We will attain greater heights.
We'll be seated with Christ in Heavenly places
And begin to see new sights.

We can't imagine the plans God has in mind
To use us in greater ways.
The Holy Spirit will begin to reveal to us
Things that were hidden from our gaze.

New vistas will open before us
That we've never seen before.
Promises that God has fulfilled
Will make our spirits soar.

Loving, working, and serving
Will new meaning attain.
With the Holy Spirit to help us
This won't even be a strain.

Our weakness in now His strength
As we walk in His will.
We'll accomplish God's plans for us
And our destiny we will fulfill.

OUR MOUTH

The disease of many is called
Diarrhea of the mouth.
Like the mighty Mississippi
That flows from north to south

It picks up mud and debris
As it travels on its way
Likewise, we pick up dirt and trivia
So, we must watch what we say.

Our words can cause harm
That tears a person down
Yet, God's Word tells us to lift them up
To free those that are bound

The more words that we speak
The less value they have to the hearer
Like a flood they bring confusion
So be precise and the meaning will be clearer

God also in His wisdom
Gave us one mouth and two ears
Everyone needs a chance
To express their joys and their fears

Even in our prayers and petitions
God knows us before we speak
So be concise and get to the point
And we'll find the answers we seek.

Before we open our mouth
Ask God for the words to speak
He will give us wisdom
As first His will we seek.

OUR RESOURCES

Money can't buy health, happiness, or peace
It is simply an illusion.
It may make life easier on earth
But at this life's final conclusion

We will all stand before God's judgment seat
Give an account of what we've been given.
What are our motives?
Are we power and greed driven?

God gives us the ability to succeed
And the results will be weighed on His scales.
He is an impartial Judge
And He already knows the details.

Have we used our resources wisely
To help those in need?
Or have we heaped it on ourselves?
Money to God, is a seed.

A seed planted in good ground
Will being a harvest we may not see.
Souls brought into the kingdom
Prisoners that were bound, set free.

If we use our money for a life of luxury
With no thought for the needy all around,
We need to stop, and take inventory
We are standing on shaky ground.

The soul's we've saved, the seeds we've sown
Those deeds that come from our heart.
These are all that remain behind
When from this earth, we depart.

Then judgment will be rendered
And it will always be fair.
Heaven or hell will be eternal
Not money, nor power, can keep us from there.

PARTNERS

Precious Holy Spirit
How wonderful you are to me.
You are my life, my peace, my love,
You make me what I ought to be.

It is the power of the exalted Jesus
Flowing unto my life through the Holy Spirit.
That is why we each must tarry
Until His power we inherit.

Now we must move forward
As He leads and directs our way.
Others will be drawn to his presence
So, keep walking forward – don't delay.

Take him with you wherever you go
Every believer needs his power.
To walk in victory in this dark world
To defeat the enemy – the devourer.

Every believer must seek to be filled
Or flounder in weakness and fear.
With Your presence within us
You reveal and make things clear.

Then tongues will naturally follow.
Our private language of prayer.
We'll walk in new boldness and power
For we are an unbeatable pair.

PIPES

Water in different parts of the country
Is a little different to our taste.
Water brings nourishment to plants and people
But a lot of it goes to waste.

The pipes that deliver the water
They are basically all alike.
The kind of water that they deliver
Is not determined by the pipe.

They are just a delivery system
And God's children are just the same.
We don't choose what He causes to flow through us,
But it brings life to others in his name.

So, we are each just a pipe
We must be clean so His water can flow
To all those who are thirsty.
And then we can watch them grow.

All of God's people are similar
He decides what flows through each one.
Each pipe is equally important
They bring growth that He has begun.

Just a cup of water to one dying
Is important beyond belief.
It brings hope into their life
And offers them sweet relief.

Let's not waste this life-giving water
So many people are thirsty and dry.
When we have the water of His Word
Let it flow – don't let them die.

PREPARATION

God toughens us in the fires of affliction.
Yet, this is not abuse.
Sometimes it is necessary
To prepare us for His use.

The enemy continually taunts us
That there is no future ahead.
You need to just end it all.
It would be better to be dead.

Yet, God has a future in mind.
That will bring much glory to His name.
Something new and different.
Nothing of the old self will remain.

New revelation and boldness
That you've never had before.
You're to go out and conquer new territory
And God will open each door.

Don't try to figure it out.
Just go forward in trust and confidence.
There will be enemies to conquer,
But your faith will be your defense.

You'll look back in childlike wonder
At what God has done through you.
You will be a fearless leader
As new visions come into view.

SATISFACTION

Satisfaction doesn't come from getting what we want
But from becoming what God designed us to be.
He already had a plan in mind
But we were blind and could not see.

We are independent and selfish
We are determined to go our own way,
Making plans that we strive to fulfill
Wondering why, when there is delay.

Our eyes are focused on self
Until we come to a block in our plan.
We try to go over it or under it.
That won't work if it is God's hand.

He is trying to get our attention
To make us stop and think.
What is really important in life?
It can vanish in a wink.

When God finally gets through to us
And we turn in the opposite direction,
We realize what is important
And we welcome God's correction.

Now He can begin to mold and shape us
For the work He has for us to do.
Life will be filled with surprises
Each day it is something new.

This was our destiny all the time
Something that we did not realize.
God knew it all the time
But to us it was a big surprise.

SEEDS

Our words are seeds.
So be careful what you sow.
When they fall to the ground.
They will begin to grow.

What will they produce?
Will they be flowers or weeds?
It all will depend.
On the character of the seeds.

Out of the abundance of the heart.
The mouth speaketh.
Whatever is stored in there
Will determine what we reapeth.

Like beautiful flowers
With sweet fragrance also
Our words can lift others up.
And help their faith to grow.

Or they can be like weeds
That choke out growth as well.
They are a hindrance to others
And often cause them to fail.

We are the ones who spread the seed,
So, let's guard our heart with care.
Someday we will receive our reward
As the harvest we will share.

Send Me

Some of the loneliest and forgotten people
Are in nursing homes and in jails,
With limited opportunity to go outside
Confined to beds, wheelchairs, or in cells.

Yet, God has not forgotten them
They are precious in His sight.
Because the enemy comes to steal, kill, and destroy
They've been robbed of their birthright.

The right to move in freedom
To enjoy life at its best.
Just the choice of which food to eat
To play, to work or to rest.

If God called you to go
Would you answer, "Send me!"?
Jesus said, "When you do it for the least of these
You have done it unto me."

SPEAK, LORD

Learn to say, "Speak, Lord"
And life will become a romance.
Our steps are ordered by the Lord
And nothing happens by chance.

Then, when we obey His voice
We will accomplish many great things.
We will walk in His presence
And the fulfillment that it brings.

Why go through life standing around
Always in the dark,
Fearful of so many things?
Satan's bite is nothing but a bark.

Too many people have chosen this path
With the fear and worry it entails.
We who know, can lift them up
And show them how love prevails.

People are precious to our Lord
He wants them all to be saved.
Satan has blinded their eyes
And now they are his slaves.

We are God's ambassadors on earth
We have the words to set them free.
The Holy Spirit is here to help us.
Now the task is up to you and me.

STAND OUT

It's easier to blend in than to stand out
Yet, we answer to a higher call.
We are a peculiar people
And we should always stand tall.

We must never compromise
Or settle for anything less.
Because we represent Christianity
And must look and do our best.

We may face adversity
But we have the Holy Spirit's power.
We can sweeten the atmosphere
Which the enemy has made sour.

Our very presence creates light
Where it was dark before.
We bring peace where there is strife
What was lost we now restore.

What a joy to live for Jesus
To bring hope where there is fear,
To lead a soul to salvation
And feel Jesus' presence near.

TESTING

Joy emerges from the ashes of adversity
When we are thankful in every situation.
Character grows when we are under pressure
This is the basis for kingdom education.

When life is always a bed of roses
We grow weak and inefficient.
We think that God is blessing us
And the little we do is sufficient.

We all must have a time of testing
To know that our faith is real.
When God is satisfied, He can trust us.
Then, the Holy Spirit applies His seal.

When our faith has passed the test of time
We recognize better the enemy's snare.
Temptation will always be a part of life
But we have learned not to go there.

Now, God's peace reigns in our lives
As we rest in His embrace
He will fight the battle for us
And He covers us with His grace.

TIME

Yesterday is history, tomorrow a mystery
But our gift from God is today.
Are we taking advantage of each opportunity?
Or do we fritter our time away

Sitting in front of the television?
At the computer just playing a game?
Time is a valuable possession
Next week won't be the same.

As we study to be workman approved
God will give us divine appointments.
Always be alert and ready for action
So, we won't be a disappointment.

We are here to bear fruit for His Kingdom
When it is eaten – we just bear some more.
When we learn to use our time wisely
We'll be more fruitful than ever before.

WALKING TOGETHER

When I promised you green pastures
I did not mean religious activity.
I desire your fellowship, not service
And a spirit of joyfulness, not negativity.

I desire also that you delight in each other
My kids should desire to play together.
Life is meant to be enjoyed
With My presence it's even better.

Together you will accomplish much more
Than when each one of you works alone.
You each one have something to contribute
I designed you to be different, not a clone.

The pleasure we share is great
When we see that a job is well done.
Much has been accomplished
And many souls have been won.

You won't realize that you've been working
You were having so much fun.
I delight to see you so excited
When we walk together as one.

WE CRY OUT

No pain lasts forever
No evil triumphs in the end.
Our God is in control
And on Him we can depend.

The world is getting more chaotic
We see it every day.
Many are filled with fear
And cannot find their way.

Murderers are really rampant
Killing everyone they see.
Souls are in bondage
That need to be set free.

Lord, we cry out to you
Help us stem this evil tide.
Under the shadow of your wings
Is the only place to hide.

Our prayers must be urgent
As we cry out in Your Name.
Give us courage and wisdom
Our loved ones to reclaim.

Time is growing shorter
Night is coming soon.
We must work while it is day
Before earth's final doom.

WHAT IT MEANS TO BE AN AMERICAN

We in America know what freedom is like
Are we praying and working for it in other lands?
Jesus made us His Ambassadors
And we are His feet and hands.

We must not take freedom for granted
For it can be taken away.
Not necessarily by outside forces
But inside by moral decay.

Selfishness is a strong human trait
It is common to all mankind.
Hearts must be changed dramatically
Before it can touch the mind.

Greed for money, power and fame
Will always stand in the way.
Only when the Holy Spirit draws men
Will they listen to what we say.

We have the words of life and liberty
As we esteem others more than self.
To see people as valuable commodity
Instead of power and wealth.

To whom much is given, much is required
And we have been blessed beyond measure.
What are we doing to impact our world?
Do we share this amazing treasure?

The knowledge that Jesus is the only way
To bring peace upon this earth.
As Christians and Americans, we have the privilege
Of sharing the secret of our new birth.

WITNESS

Adding souls to God's kingdom
To witness is our task.
But how will we ever know
If we are too timid to ask?

The question "Do you know Jesus?"
The answer will be no or yes.
If the answer is yes
Share together how you've been blessed.

If the answer is no
Then just share the Good News.
You have planted a seed
Now, they accept or they refuse.

If they say, "I go to Church."
This is a good place to start.
Explain the difference in head knowledge
And letting Jesus reign in your heart.

Either way you have made the effort
You've given them something to think about.
This brings praise and honor to God
So, the stones don't have to cry out.

WORKING

Are we working for God or with God?
There is a difference, you see.
Do we think we are smart enough
To fix people and things like they should be?

Do we plan and even work diligently
To fulfill our own agenda,
When in reality we are in the way
And the Holy Spirit's work we hinder.

We need to seek God's will
Then He will give us the words to say
To minister and exhort someone
To show them the narrow way.

Jesus, our Head, is in control
We are His hands and His feet.
As we pray for wisdom and discernment
He'll show us the tares and the wheat.

Only the Holy Spirit can draw men
And only He knows when they are ready.
Fools rush in unprepared
So just remain calm and steady.

Then when the time is right
God will show us who and when.
Then we can work with Jesus
Another soul for His kingdom, to win.

Working With, Not For

It is so much easier for us to do something ourselves
Than to put our trust in God alone.
With just a little more faith or Bible study
The enemy's influence we think we can postpone.

There are so many people working for God
And so few of us working with Him.
No wonder we fall so short of success
And the number of converts is slim.

When we learn to listen like Jesus did
And only do what the Father says to do.
We'll be surprised at the results
It will be amazing and something new.

Only the Father knows a person's heart
And what it will take to succeed.
If we'll just be patient and wait on Him
He will fulfill someone's every need.

We wouldn't have wasted so much time and energy
To accomplish what only God can do through us.
It is hard to believe what we have done
Without all that bother and fuss.

WORTHY

I'm separating My sheep from unworthy sheep
Those whose hearts are totally Mine.
I will light up the dark hidden places
Those in deception will be left behind.

Things are going to get much worse
Before that final day draws near
When My wrath will be loosed
And men will be overcome with fear.

But those who are sold out to Me
Need not fear what lies ahead.
I will protect those of Mine
They will be clothed and fed.

The final harvest is on the horizon
Some Christians fool themselves, but not Me.
For they are Christians in name only
Their hearts are fickle and not worthy.

So, take heed and redeem this time
Keep your heart pure, and your mind clear.
Witness to everyone that I put in your path
And I'll deliver those you hold dear.

WRONG MOTIVES

If we do things for God with the wrong motives
They will be wood, hay, and stubble.
When we think that we've done something great
It will probably bring sorrow and trouble.

Too much of what the world thinks is great
Is as filthy rags in God's sight.
He rewards the humble in heart
Who really strive to do things right.

It's probable someone of lowly esteem
Will be rewarded the most.
Someone who feels he's done nothing for God
Instead of those of whom the world will boast.

It is not in works, but in fellowship
That we feel fulfilled indeed.
In doing the task God tells us to do
We'll be filling someone else's need.

It's the meek and lowly in heart
Who are happiest in the long run.
While those who try to do it all
Never seem to get it done.

Many miss out on God's blessings
For He should be our source.
He hopes we will learn from our mistakes
But He will never resort to force.

YOUTH
Isaiah 41:9-10

Those who have ears – open them and hear
I am calling to My youth
Those that are far away
And those that are near.

I'm preparing you for the end-time crusade,
For the time is drawing near.
Earth's birth pangs are getting stronger,
And many will be filled with fear.

I've filled you with My strength and courage
So you are able to stand strong.
My right hand will uphold you
And I'll put you right where you belong.

You won't even feel the fiery darts
That the enemy sends each day.
When others run to and fro
You'll wait and follow My way.

You'll be an example for each generation
That I, your God, am in control.
You will lead many to My cross
Because I've made you bold.

I AM
SPEAKING

TO MY CHILDREN

TEMPTATION

ABUNDANCE

Do we realize we are robbing God
When we withhold the tithe?
It all is His and He is the one
Who makes us come alive.

He gives us gifts and talents
He gives us the ability to work.
When we hold on to what is His
We are acting like a jerk.

God only asks for a tenth
We get to keep all of the rest.
How we spend it is up to us
We can waste it or feather our nest.

When we enjoy blessing others
We are generous and give even more.
We can't out give God
We'll have more than ever before.

Jesus promises us abundant life
This includes security and health.
He gives us love, mercy, and grace
These can't be bought with wealth.

Many who are rich in this world
Are miserable and commit suicide.
They worshipped money instead of God
And their spirit never came alive.

ACCOLADES

Don't exchange the approval of God
For the accolades of men.
The devil is sly and shrewd
And this battle he wants to win.

With promises of fame or riches
He may deceive even the elect.
It seems to make a lot of sense
But it may cause your life to wreck.

When you are undecided, wait
Until you have God's direction.
He sees the pitfalls ahead
And He is your protection.

Men's accolades will puff us up
And then pride can come in.
It's best to suffer for a little while
For it's God we serve in the end.

AMBITION

Ambition for money will make you greedy
For you always want to have more.
Then things you begin to accumulate
Will surely open the door

To the enemy who will use them
To draw you away from Me.
Things will become the chains
That will keep you from being free.

Ambition for pleasure will make you indulgent
Thinking it's always about me.
"I deserve to be entertained"
Then your eyes are blinded – you do not see.

I want My children to have fun,
But you are fulfilled more when you serve.
It's not by receiving but by giving
That blessings come that you didn't deserve.

Ambition for recognition will make you self-indulgent.
Then, you think too highly of yourself.
I am the only one who can promote you
I give you the ability to succeed and gain wealth.

So, when you think you have done it all
This will always lead to pride.
That is an abomination in My sight
And I may simply put you aside.

When you learn to think correctly of yourself
And realize that I am in control,
You'll fulfill the plans I have for you
And they will be something to behold.

Beware

I don't want any child of Mine
Dabbling in witchcraft, no matter how innocent it seems.
If I want to tell you something
I will speak or give you visions and dreams.

Books like the Harry Potter Series
Astrology charts, palm reading too.
Tend to lead you astray
And away from My word, which is true.

Just a little crack in your spiritual armor
Will let the enemy come in.
The he will confuse your thoughts
And lead you into sin.

You must be constantly on your guard.
Renew your mind with My Word each day.
For the Devil is patiently waiting
To find a way to lead you astray.

It's hard once you are headed in the wrong direction
To turn yourself around.
There are lures and temptation at every turn
Enticements to sin truly abound.

It's so much better to stay focused
Keep My word uppermost in your mind.
Don't even glance at temptation
Always looking at Jesus – never looking behind.

CHANGE

If we really want to change
God will move mountains to help us.
He looks on our heart, He sees our motives
Is He filled with delight or a frown of disgust?

Are we comfortable with our sin?
Something we don't want to give up?
We feel it's something we deserve
It's not really that corrupt.

Many others are doing it too
So, it can't be that bad.
As Christians we're held to a higher standard
We're not free to follow each new fad.

We should be an example to others
That Jesus is all we need.
Many rejoice to see Christians in sin
So, we must guard every word and deed.

We grieve the Holy Spirit
When our actions betray His trust.
We must repent and ask forgiveness
For succumbing to carnal lust.

God forgives, but we must make restitution
For the damage we've done to His Name.
Live our lives in love and purity
Forever steadfast to remain.

Destructive Forces

Anxiety produces tension
And tension leads to pain.
Worry is a destructive force
Why allow it to remain?

Fear is devastating to the physical body
Anger throws poison in the mix.
Most arthritis is brought on by unforgiveness
Asthma by suppressed fury that is hard to fix.

Hidden sin is revealed by maladies of the body
Be sure your sin will find you out.
We need to repent and change our thoughts
Be filled with faith instead of doubt

When you have complete confidence in Me
In My loving, trusting, care.
You won't ever have to face things alone
For I promised that I would always be there

Your thoughts must be controlled by self-discipline
What you sow in your secret thought life you shall reap.
Sow generosity, forgiveness, hope, and praise
Your days will be satisfied and your nights with sweet sleep.

DOUBLE TROUBLE

The Devil knows his time is short
So, his efforts now are double.
He seeks to discourage God's children
He does it with hardship and with trouble.

He uses sickness and problems
He tries this to break us down.
But He who is in us is greater
So no doubt in us is to be found.

We will rejoice in our tribulations
Knowing we will overcome.
With the blood of the Lamb and our testimony
We know where our victory comes from.

Our God will fight the battle for us
He does this when we step aside.
The enemy's plans will be suppressed
No longer can he hide.

As we fast, praise, and worship
We'll rise to the occasion
And see the Devil routed
From this his intended invasion.

FOOLS

There are young fools and old fools
Not one who is mentally defective.
Others can't make you a fool
You choose, for it is elective.

Pati is one Biblical word for a fool
It is the description of an attitude.
Fools don't welcome instruction or correction
They have no sense of gratitude.

A hardened fool, *Kesil*
Is thickheaded, sluggish, and obstinate.
They think they know it all
And are often filled with hate.

A mocking fool, *Letz* is a scoffer
Making fun of everything.
They don't realize life is serious
And the destruction this can bring.

The denying fool, *Nabal*
The one who says in his heart
There is no God
He's in hell when from earth he does depart.

Those who disregard moral and spiritual values
Are foolish or acting in what we call folly.
They scoff at the idea of Heaven
So, at life's end they miss the trolly.

Some fools are just stupid
They destroy and consume.
Many are heedless even wicked
Unless changed they face certain doom.

Some people are just silly
Always acting like a fool.
They haven't been paying attention
And have become the enemy's tool.

So, don't choose to be a fool
Make Jesus your Lord and friend.
This is the essence of wisdom
And Heaven is our ultimate end.

FRAGRANCE

God loves us enough to work on us for a lifetime
What a precious thought.
He never gives up, but keeps improving.
Are we growing as we ought?

God disciplines us so we share His holiness
He is taking us from glory to glory.
As we give our lives to His service
We will all have a story.

A story to share with others
That will help them grow and bloom.
Together we are His garden
That is filled with sweet perfume.

It's the fragrance of life to those who listen
Of death to those who refuse to believe.
When people don't choose to come to Jesus
It causes our hearts to grieve.

But God has given us each free will
And we have the privilege to choose.
Will we spend eternity with Jesus?
Or will we our salvation lose?

IT'S SNEAKY

Pride is often sneaky
It creeps in unaware.
When you think you've done a great job
It's time to become aware.

Pride is creeping in
Stop it at the door.
If Satan can get his foot in
He'll take up even more.

Applause is flattering to the ego
But it is fraught with danger.
It is even more appealing
When it comes from a stranger.

So always remind yourself
You are simply a lowly pipe.
God chooses what flows through you
He can cut if off with a single swipe.

So, lift each success as a bouquet to God
Give honor and glory where it is due.
When you remember where your gift comes from
God will keep on using you.

ITCHING EARS

Do we want a cost-less, cross-less, reproof-less, gospel?
Do we have itching ears today?
Preachers who promise prosperity and sunshine
When we send our money their way.

God's word teaches us that hardship grows character.
Persecution will put us on our knees.
God always hears our heartfelt cry
He honors a heart that grieves.

Over the sins of our Nation
We have turned our backs on His Name.
So, sin and violence run rampant
Christians are viewed with disdain.

We must reproach, reprove, and exhort
Bring lost souls into the fold.
God is giving us a little more time
To reap a harvest is our goal.

The enemy is working overtime
He knows his time is short.
We have God's word and the Spirit's power
His evil plans we can abort.

God always has a remnant
We are loyal, we trust, and obey.
Evil may triumph temporarily
But righteousness will win one day.

JUSTIFY

When things are a little shady
People are quick to try to justify.
The question is such a simple one
Is this the truth or is it a lie?

The answer is usually wordy
It comes with lots of explanation.
To cover the enemy's plot
And bring us some temptation.

Only the wise will see through the maze
To recognize the true matter at hand.
It takes work and investigation
Before you will fully understand.

This is a plan of the enemy
It's to lead many Christians astray.
You will face a massive roadblock
And encounter delay after delay.

But if God has put this truth in your heart
Don't give up; just persevere.
Time and circumstances will reveal the truth
And finally make things clear.

God knows exactly what's taking place
And you are His watchman on the wall.
Relax and let the Holy Spirit lead.
For you heard and answered God's call.

MAKE BELIEVE

Make-believe Christians
Will eventually show their real colors.
Whatever their social status
Even if they are fathers or mothers.

They know the words to say
And know how to play the part.
But they haven't surrendered to Jesus
And He knows what's in their heart.

Others are not so discerning
They think that they are born again.
So, they are really shocked.
To see them fall into sin.

God loves them so much.
He tries to win them back.
But He has given them free choice
And this is an established fact.

God's hands are tied
They have chosen their path.
So, instead of His love
They will taste His wrath.

NEGATIVITY

When all you talk about is negative
You are living in the gutter.
It's called a sin in the Bible
When we complain and we mutter.

If we really believe that God is in control
Then we'll rejoice and pray without ceasing.
God's word plainly tells us
That in the end times evil is ever increasing.

We fight evil with good
Not by stirring up trouble.
If you always talk about the bad
Your anxiety will only double.

Try to seek out the good around
Encourage others with words of praise,
Always trusting God has a plan
Then peace and joy will fill your days.

OUR THOUGHTS

Our thoughts are like soldiers
The battlefield is our mind.
The enemy uses fiery darts
In order to make us blind.

Then he sends in his troops
His thoughts to put in place.
We think the thoughts are our own
But this is not the case.

The enemy has infiltrated our mind
He wants to steal our faith.
He sends his evil thoughts
But we have opened the gate.

God tells us to take our thoughts captive
Or they will flourish and grow.
Then we do something really stupid
Which will always delight our foe.

Let's take time to examine our thoughts
Will they bring good, or cause loss?
Will they draw someone closer to Jesus?
We need to count the cost.

Thoughts always lead to action
And there are consequences to pay.
When troubling thoughts control us
This is the time to pray.

God tells us to ask for wisdom
We need it to protect our mind.
God loves us and wants the best for us
So true happiness we can find.

Overflowing

Do not go out in the morning
With a closed, unhearing ear.
But be always listening and seeking
So that we are always ready to hear

The voice of our God speaking
Through the beauty we see all around us.
A sunrise, a butterfly, or a flower
But quietness is a must.

Love is the core of life
From it all other things spring forth.
The supply will never cease
For it is God who is our source.

Always move upward and forward
Movement gives purpose to life and its beauty.
It's the overflow of our love
So, it is never just a duty.

We are made in God's image
So, we are all to be creative.
It can be ignored, choked, or twisted
By indifference even negated.

God desires that we flow in divine life,
But if dammed up, it becomes a dead sea.
Weakness and frustration will result
Until Jesus comes to set us free.

His presence results in overflowing joy
As we become a co-laborer in God's work.
The results are great beyond measure
And anyone who refuses is a jerk.

Paper Idol

Pagans worshipped an idol of gold
Today we worship one of paper.
We depend on the government or almighty dollar
Instead of depending on our Maker.

We look up to others with wealth
As though they have achieved something great.
God's Word tells us the love of money is a bad root
It can lead to envy and hate.

If we have God's wisdom in our heart
And use our resources to help others in need,
Then God will bless us with more
As we sow, He supplies the seed.

If we keep God on the throne of our life
He will use us in mighty ways
To accomplish His work He started on earth
In spite of the enemy's delays.

When we put aside all other idols
And worship our Maker instead,
Our lives will be a blessing to others
We've surrendered control – we are Spirit led.

Persevere

If we are making inroads into the enemy's territory
He mounts an aggressive attack.
He sends sickness or trouble in our family
He is always working behind our back.

When people are involved in our endeavor
He puts roadblocks in their way.
Anything to get them distracted
With delay after delay.

He wants us to become discouraged
To lose our passion and our zeal.
But we know that God has called us
So, it does not matter how we feel.

We must continue to carry on
With perseverance and determination.
We'll go over or around the roadblocks
To reach our destination.

We know great victory lies ahead
When we come under strong attack.
God's authority will slowly overcome
He will give us what we lack.

We rejoice in tribulation
Knowing we'll win in the end.
We'll glorify our Father above
For on Him, we can depend.

REJECTION

The spirit of rejection is one of the worst
It causes agony of the soul.
It can take away all identity
It makes us feel we're not whole.

Whatever the cause may be
It is not entirely our fault.
The enemy has found an entry
And the battle is a full assault.

Only Jesus Christ holds the answer
It is when we decide to let Him in.
He will heal those wounds of self-esteem
And help us to feel complete again.

Only our pride will hold us back
As we hate to admit defeat.
But the burden is too heavy to carry
We must lay it at Jesus' feet.

As we forgive the one who rejected us
And ask God to heal them as well.
He will reveal new vistas before us
For God has lifted the veil.

Now we can begin to heal
Embrace new ideas and plans
Life will take on new meaning
For God holds us in His hands.

SELF-PITY

No sin is worse than the sin of self-pity
It removes God from the throne of our lives.
It leaves us naked and vulnerable
In this environment the enemy thrives.

Satan makes you think
That God has abandoned you.
God may be silent, but He is always there
So just the opposite is true.

We are told to take that thought captive
And then cast it out of our mind.
Satan is the father of lies
He disturbs you so peace you can't find.

God will reach to the last grain of sand
And the remotest star to bless us once more.
All He asks is that we trust and obey
He'll pour out His blessing like never before.

Don't let the thought "poor me"
Try to lodge itself in your brain.
Start giving of yourself to others
Then true fulfillment you will gain.

SELF–RIGHTEOUS

Self-righteousness
Is an abomination
Always having to be right
Regardless of the situation.

We all fall short of the glory of God
There is no exception.
We have just opened ourselves
To the enemy's deception.

Everyone has a right to their opinion
But things should be open to debate.
Others may have keener insight
They may be better equipped to relate

To the situation at hand
It may need a different perspective.
In spite of our opinion
We should be more receptive.

We won't let the enemy control our actions
For Jesus is the one we need.
He is wisdom personified
And in the right direction He will lead.

Then, peace will reign in our sphere
When we give up our self-righteousness.
For everyone will feel they are needed
So, in victory we have reaped success.

SELFISHNESS

A selfish and self-centered life
Is one of the saddest lives on earth.
No real goals for the future
No fulfillment and no mirth.

Always having to have your way
With no thought of people around.
Only thinking of your own desires
No happiness in you can be found.

No desire to do for others
Only thinking of what you need.
Yet you are never satisfied
Your heart is full of greed.

No evidence of the Fruit of the Spirit
No love, joy, peace, or self-control.
Long-suffering? You must be kidding
Assertiveness is your goal.

A life filled with envy and jealousy
At the happiness and success of those you see.
Yet, we all have the choice in life
To be bound or to be set free.

Only in losing your life can it be found
The Bible makes this plain.
With loving and doing for others
Can one true happiness attain.

Spirit of Grief

A spirit of grief is a fearful thing
It keeps you from moving ahead.
It's not something that I admire
For a part of you is dead.

To the things I have for you to do
The life that I have planned.
You keep getting stuck in your grief
And don't heed My command.

To always be moving forward
Into a life filled with My goal.
You'll be surprised what I do through you
It will be something to behold.

There is a time for grieving
When a loved one has come home.
But if you believe in Heaven
Then you'll never feel alone.

Let go of your grief
Release it unto Me.
Then your burden will be lighter
On this we can agree.

You'll see things so much better
For your spirit's been let loose.
You'll bring much glory and honor to Me
For that grief was like a noose.

STRESS

Don't let time become a tyrant
That totally controls your life.
You keep going around in circles
Searching for peace, but nothing will suffice.

If the enemy cannot stop you
He gets behind, to push you faster.
The faster you run – the more behind you get
Now life has become a disaster.

It's time to sit down and regroup
Before depression can come in.
Ask the Holy Spirit for guidance
On His wisdom you can depend.

God tells us to seek His Kingdom first
Other things will fall into place.
God will tell you when to say no
So, your talents don't go to waste.

If you determine to start your day with prayer
He is faithful to show you the way.
To be efficient and redeem your time
Help you stay focused and calm each day.

You can't afford to keep running this way
For stress takes a terrible toll.
God wants His children healthy and happy
In body, spirit, and soul.

THE PRODIGAL

Father, you care about the prodigal
Who has wandered so far away.
They made the choice to leave
And won't listen to what we say.

They want to live their own life
Doing their own thing,
Not realizing the hurt they cause
While they are having this fling.

They don't see the darkness around them
The enemy has blinded their eyes.
The Father's love is still there.
It's just something they don't realize.

They have wandered into their own world,
And don't hear a word we say.
But we have a secret weapon
And that is when we pray.

God tells us in His Word
Fervent prayer availeth much.
No matter how hardened the heart
It will feel the Father's touch.

He will welcome them home again
With His arms opened wide.
Heaven and earth will rejoice
When the prodigal returns to our side.

TIME WAITING

The waiting time is always the testing time
Will we grow impatient and can't wait?
Thinking God is not doing anything
So, we've fallen for the enemy's bait.

We want things accomplished now
God has all the time it takes.
While we count the minutes passing by
We're wasting time, something man hates.

Sometimes our clocks and watches are a curse
We miss out on so much God has to share.
The beauty around us, the people we meet
Little touches from God that show us His care.

Many of us will fail the test of waiting
We're programmed by the world time to not waste.
We miss out on so much of God's best
As we participate in this hectic life's race.

God desires that we stop and rest awhile
As we enjoy spending time with Him in fellowship.
This alone is pleasing to our Father
It is also our highest form of worship.

Too Much Candy

At times we need a hard word from the Lord
Too much candy will make us sick.
We may be on the wrong track
And His word comes to convict.

We may need to repent or forgive
To leave the friends we are with.
We may not see the danger ahead
So, our focus may need to shift.

Why do dogs return to their vomit?
That sounds so repulsive to us.
Yet, it's the same with destructive habits
Like alcohol, drugs, or lust.

God loves and cares for His children
Many times, we feel His reproof.
It is meant to cleanse and purify us
We may need to face the truth.

We've wandered off the path of righteousness
So, let's humble ourselves and repent.
The words that we thought were harsh
Have actually been Heaven sent.

WAR'S RESULT

Politicians are the ones who initiate war
They don't care how many lives are lost.
Their greed for money and power
No matter what the cost.

The ordinary citizens bear the burden
They suffer the heartache and pain.
Loved ones lost or traumatized for life
And their lives will never be the same.

It's the people with wealth
Who back the side they want to win.
They think they can control things
But where have they been?

They are not God, and He is in control
So, they are in for a rude awakening.
When their wealth and power disappear
It will leave them simply quaking.

They did not fear man or God
And put their trust in the wrong place.
Now they have lost it all
They are standing before God face to face.

We each will stand before His judgment seat
And give an account of all we have done.
Did we gain riches and power for ourselves?
Or did we bring honor to Jesus – His Son?

The verdict will be just
For God sees the motive behind the motion.
Some will enter His perfect rest
For other separation will be their portion.

I AM
SPEAKING

To Unbelievers

INVITATION

A STUMBLING STONE OR A ROCK

Jesus is to you, either a stumbling stone
Or a rock you build your house upon.
He is a firm foundation
Father, Spirit, Son.

He is a stumbling stone
If in Him you don't believe.
His death and forgiveness
You did not receive.

He died for us all
But the choice is your own.
You think you are in control
Your will is seated on the throne.

Then when things fall apart
And you don't know where to turn.
The Holy Spirit is calling you
He doesn't want to see you burn.

All you have to do is repent
Begin to walk another way.
Jesus is waiting for you
He'll welcome you home to stay.

Depends On Us

As the end time draws nearer,
We must depend on God each day.
We can't depend on money or people.
People are selfish, money can vanish away.

Only God can see into the future.
And He promised to never leave or forsake us.
No matter how difficult things may become.
His mercy is kind and just.

As terrorism becomes more prevalent.
We are not to hide in fear.
Our God is still in control.
And He is always near.

He expects us to stand strong.
To reflect Jesus in every situation.
When we see a need, or even danger.
We step forward without hesitation.

God has to depend on His children.
To show the world that He cares.
When we stand up for truth and justice.
It's the difference between wheat and tares.

FOLLOW ME

I am the Way, the Truth and the Life
There is no other route.
Peace and joy are found in Me
Isn't that what life is about?

There is a void inside of you
That you seek to fill with work or pleasure.
But there is still emptiness inside
For these are not life's true treasure.

Only an intimate relationship with Me
Will ever make you content.
So, stand strong in My power
That no enemy can rend.

Out of our relationship
New creativity will flow.
Your life will be filled with meaning
That will begin to show.

People will be drawn to you
Just like a magnet will draw iron.
This is now your opportunity
To lead them up to Zion.

They will encounter My presence there
Like they've never felt it before.
You've fulfilled the plan I had for you
And I will cause your spirit to soar.

Far above this earthly place
Into heavenly places with Me.
You'll be filled with wonder and awe
For from earth's sorrows I've set you free.

God's Offer

Is it really all that easy?
It seems too good to be true.
The blessing and forgiveness
God offers to me and you.

We're used to working and taking
To rest and receive it all?
Believe God's Word is true
Answer when our name He does call.

My love for you is deeper than a canyon
Higher than the highest star.
Closer than the breath you breathe
Sweeter than a candy bar.

I made you in My image
Close friendship to achieve.
I loved you enough to give you free choice
To depart or believe.

JUDGMENT BY A RIGHTEOUS GOD

Only the Lord can be a righteous judge
For He looks on a person's heart.
He knows the circumstances of their life
And each influence that played a part.

In shaping and molding them
On the path that they have trod.
Whether their parents were good or bad
If unbelievers or committed to God.

We see only the results of their actions
And don't even consider the cause.
We are quick to observe and judge
They have rebelled or broken our laws.

We may have done something far worse
Had we but walked in their shoes.
God has blessed us with His mercy
So, the good way was easy to choose.

Let's lay aside our judgmental attitude
Embrace them with love and grace
Help them on their way to salvation
This will put a smile on God's face.

No Hiding

Lord, You still love us
Even in our wanderings or evil intent.
Your love remains steadfast
For it is set in cement.

Even to the vilest sinner
And the self-righteous saint.
You relentlessly pursue us
You never grow weary and faint.

There is no place to hide from You
Not in Heaven nor on earth.
You made us in Your image
And our souls are of matchless worth.

Even when we turn our backs on you
You never give up on us.
You draw us until our final breath on earth
And Your judgment is always just.

You give us every opportunity to change
To repent and return to You
You welcome us with open arms
Both the Gentile and the Jew.

Our Treasure

Why not store up treasure in Heaven instead of on earth
For then it will last through eternity.
Treasure on earth can vanish in a heartbeat
There is so much uncertainty.

Those who have wealth never have enough
They are always striving for more.
Yet, so many times they are not as happy
As those who are simply poor.

Things can never satisfy our soul
They just bring temporary joy.
Depending on them is foolish
For the enemy can quickly destroy.

When our foundation is built on Jesus
We will stand firm in every trial.
The enemy is a master deceiver
But with the mind of Christ he can't beguile.

So, as we continue to stand in faith
Our treasure will be multiplied.
The fruit we bear in life
Will lift Jesus up to be glorified.

Return

God's love is undeserved but unchanging
Often ignored but never withdrawn.
No matter how far we've wandered
Or how many things we've done wrong.

Just as the Father welcomed the prodigal
He welcomes His own who return.
His love will cover a multitude of sins
It is something that we can't earn.

Even if we've run to a far country
We'll always find welcome waiting.
So repent and turn around
Decide now, no more debating.

We will never face rejection
Our Father's love is beyond comprehension.
When He sees us coming from afar
We'll have His undivided attention.

There is safety in the Father's love
Found nowhere else on earth.
He lavishes it on His children
For each one is of infinite worth.

TODAY

All of creation recognizes the Savior
Why then do people still not believe?
It's because they follow the devil
He is the one who comes to deceive.

He always works in the darkness
He stays hidden from our view.
His tactics are as old as creation
He doesn't know anything new.

Even the rocks will praise Jesus
All creation awaits His return.
Yet He freely offers salvation to mankind.
It's a gift that we don't have to earn.

Many had rather believe a lie
Than to recognize what is true.
Following Jesus is the only way to Heaven
Today, He's inviting you.

WE MATTER

Every person matters in God's sight
For He sees the potential in us.
We have to learn to listen to His voice
Then obedience is a must.

Then we can rise above our circumstances
No matter how hopeless they seem.
Determination and self-control are necessary
If we want to fulfill our dream.

God puts people and situations in our lives
To help us to mature.
The enemy will shoot fiery darts
Seemingly more than we can endure.

But with the Holy Spirit's help
We can overcome all odds.
Our eyes must stay fixed upon Jesus
For in this world there are many false gods.

Then we will blossom and bear fruit
If we refuse to grow weary or fall.
Then, God will be so proud of us
We have persevered and fulfilled His call.

I AM
SPEAKING

TO UNBELIEVERS

THE STEPS INTO GOD'S PRESENCE

The Steps Into God's Presence

The path is a mix of rising steps and plateaus,
but always upward.

There are 8 steps:

1. Repentance
2. Salvation
3. Baptism
4. Justification
5. Sanctification
6. Obedience
7. Holiness
8. Judgment

We're free to choose
To win, to lose
One will prevail
Be it Heaven or Hell

REPENTANCE

When we begin our walk with God
Repentance is the first step we take.
We realize we are a sinner
And our very life is at stake.

We all sin and fall short of God's glory
We just have to recognize this fact.
Satan has blinded our eyes
We've been on earth's fast track.

We need to stop and take a breather
And realize what's important in life.
Do we want to live in peace?
Or continue in turmoil and strife?

Jesus is the only answer
We must come humbly to His Cross.
Exchange filthy rags for a robe of righteousness
His purity for all of our dross.

He's already paid the price in full
What do we have to lose?
A life filled with light and expectancy
He leaves it up to us to choose.

SALVATION

It is called the Roman Road to Salvation
And it's open to everyone.
God does not desire that any should perish
That's why He sent His only Son.

We all sin and fall short of the glory of God
But He has provided a way to escape.
When we make Jesus Lord of our life
He is the Way, through Heaven's gate.

Now when God looks down on us
He sees us covered in Jesus' righteousness.
We don't look the same anymore
We have taken on Jesus' likeness.

It's up to us to work on our flesh
We should grow more like Jesus each day.
We are held to a higher standard
In all that we do and say.

So, we continue to study and mature
Build the character of an adult, not a child.
Then, the joy of pleasing our Father
Will make all of our efforts worthwhile.

BAPTISM

Baptism is an outward sign
Of an inward turn-around.
Instead of self, Jesus is Lord of our life
New peace and purpose we have found

It's a public declaration
To all our family and friends
That the years of wasting our lives
Have finally come to an end.

We now have a new purpose in life
To bear fruit for the master's use.
To live our life, an example for others
Drugs and drink were just an excuse.

To deny our responsibilities
Live each day just pleasing me.
Now we know how much time we've wasted
For Jesus has opened our eyes to see

The pain to those around us
Who are lost and have not a clue.
That God loves them and has a plan for their lives
He'll help make their dreams come true.

When we come up out of the water
We are born again, a new creature indeed.
Now the ground in our heart is ready
To receive His Gospel – the seed.

As we study and read God's Word
The seed will grow and flourish.
Now we are ready to go out
To those seeds in others nourish.

What unspeakable joy, to have a new start
To live life to the fullest each day.
We know the Holy Spirit is guiding us
Giving us the words to say.

Now as we join our hearts together
We can make a difference in the place we live.
We've grown in wisdom and knowledge
Now let's go out there and give!

JUSTIFIED

We are justified by faith
Just like Abraham.
When we die to ourselves daily
We bring glory to the great I AM.

When our lives are poured out for others
We are precious in God's sight.
He opens more doors of opportunity
To do His will is our delight.

Others will be drawn to our light
Just as moths are drawn to a flame.
We have on our mantle of authority
When we do it all in Jesus' name.

Our lives will take on new meaning
We are fulfilling our destiny.
Joy will radiate like sunbeams
And we'll soar like eagles, so free!

The things of this world will grow dim
For our eyes are fixed on things above.
We are seated with Jesus in Heavenly places
And surrounded with His peace and love

SANCTIFIED

Sanctified is to be set apart
Different from those around.
We are walking together with Jesus
And this is Holy Ground.

We are now a peculiar people
An instrument in the Master's hand,
Sent out like sheep among wolves
To declare salvation in this land.

The message of good news we bring
Will set others free from sin.
When they listen and accept this message
They will be born again.

Then they will be part of God's army
To announce and perform His Word.
We will raise up a shout together
Over the clamor of this world – it is heard.

All men will be given the opportunity
To repent and be saved like us.
They can look forward to their glorified body
When the old one returns to dust.

OBEDIENCE

Obedience is better than sacrifice
I expect you to obey.
My Word is yea and amen
Yours should be the same way.

A man's word reflects on his name
So always stand by what you say.
It is a witness to unbelievers
That integrity is the better way.

You represent Me in this world
Living epistles written on your heart.
Others see the way you behave
And that's what sets you apart.

When others panic and you are calm
They will begin to wonder why?
When you have Jesus in your heart
You are not afraid to die.

To willingly lay down your life for others
Is obedience to My command.
I'm in charge of the situation
No one can snatch you out of My hand.

HOLINESS

Holiness is the balance between my nature
And the law of God as expressed by Jesus Christ.
I must fight to keep myself pure
For Jesus has already paid a very high price.

Lord, time spent in Your presence
Is time that is never wasted.
For we are feeding our spirit-man
New thoughts that have never been tasted.

It is only Jesus living in me
That makes holiness possible at all.
For man's nature is sinful
This was a result of the fall.

But Jesus living in me
Makes me holy in God's sight.
I can rest in this revelation
For now, I reveal His light.

JUDGMENT

If we have an intimate relationship with Jesus
Then we have nothing to fear.
We can look forward with anticipation
When Judgment Day draws near.

We will stand before our Maker
Not accompanied by others, but all alone.
He will open the Book of Remembrance
From His position on the Great White Throne.

The things we've accomplished, good or bad
Will be remembered once more.
Many will be wood, hay, and stubble
Hopefully there will be jewels galore.

We will then receive our crowns
For the work on earth we have done,
Both the big and small things
That brought honor to His Son.

Climbing Upward

We are going from glory to glory
In our spiritual walk,
Sometimes gaining new knowledge
Sometimes just empty talk.

Little by little, precept upon precept
Ever climbing toward the top.
At times, seated in Heavenly places
Other times at a complete stop.

But our efforts are not in vain
For our Father takes note when we try.
He knows our flesh is weak
That's why Jesus had to die.

When we are weak, He is our strength
And when we reach the end of our rope.
He is the one to lift us up
To fill us with new hope.

Our destiny is clear in His Word
And we mature in each step that we take.
Our reward will be The Crown of Life
It all depends on the decisions we make.

I AM
SPEAKING

To Unbelievers

THE ENEMY'S WORK

A DIFFERENCE

When we commit a sin
We have missed the mark.
We failed to recognize Jesus
And so, we wander in the dark.

Iniquity is another matter
It is an unrighteous wrong.
We've wounded another person
Who was weak instead of strong.

Transgression is open rebellion
It is labeled as witchcraft in the Word.
We have disobeyed God's law.
That all of our lives we've heard.

All sin is rooted in pride
When we think we know it all,
When, in fact, we are ignorant,
And pride goes before a fall.

So, be hesitant to judge others
Just look in the mirror and see.
We each are guilty and need forgiveness
And that also includes me.

God is faithful to forgive our sin
When we repent and ask Him to.
Then, we can move forward in confidence
Knowing we'll make it through.

DARKNESS

As long as things are in the dark
The enemy can take us at his will.
He sends shameful thoughts to embarrass us
Our self-esteem he wants to kill.

But once it is brought into the light
No matter how bad the sin.
God can begin the healing
Just ask forgiveness and let Him begin.

The enemy always operates in the dark
For light exposes evil deeds.
It's wise to stop thoughts early
Before they are planted – evil seeds.

That's why Gods Word tells us
To cast down thoughts and renew our mind.
It's a constant daily battle
But that's how true freedom, we can find.

DEPENDENT

God enables and empowers
But He never enslaves us.
He knows our human weakness.
For He fashioned us from dust.

We are dependent on the Holy Spirit.
For each and every endeavor.
When we surrender ourselves completely,
This relationship no enemy can sever.

We are the only ones
Who can take ourselves out of God's Hand,
When we willfully turn our backs on Jesus
And think we, by ourselves, can stand.

We have become our own worst enemies.
And we may be headed straight for hell.
Life on earth will also be miserable.
Peace and contentment we've abandoned as well.

There is a place inside us.
That can only be filled by God alone.
We can try everything else on earth.
But we are flesh of His flesh and bone of His bone.

We may as well surrender now.
And find that joy it brings.
Jesus will be our all in all.
Instead of all those other things.

OUR ENEMIES

Father, help me not to turn up my nose
at the whiff of other's sin
While ignoring the stench of my own
Open my eyes to see me as you see me.
Is pride seated on the throne?

We are so quick to judge others
When the plank is in our own eye.
If we've not walked in their shoes
We can't hear their silent cry.

You've told us to love our enemies
To pray for mercy for them too.
We've received what we didn't deserve
Love and forgiveness from You.

Our love and mercy may turn them around
And open their ears to hear
The Holy Spirit wooing them
Calling their name, drawing them near.

We are Jesus' here on earth
And this battle we will win.
As we love in spite of persecution
And our enemy becomes our friend.

PORNOGRAPHY

The problem of pornography is high in our nation
It saturates your soul with sin.
When you open the door to the enemy
This battle will be hard to win.

Pictures in your mind are hard to erase
Visualization is a powerful thing.
On the internet it is easy and private
You thought it was a casual fling

Into something that might be interesting
Then you are drawn into the enemy's snare.
He wants to corrupt you inside and out
With a burden that is hard to share.

Too many start viewing it at an early age
When their curiosity is at its peak.
With parental guidance missing at home
The enemy preys on those who are weak.

Even Pastors and Christians
Can be caught up in this web of deceit.
The only place of safety
Is found at our Savior's feet.

Only as you confess to family and friends
Can this problem be brought to the light.
Then ask for God's forgiveness
And He will help you win this fight.

SEXUAL SIN

Adultery and fornication are major sins
Because our body is the temple of God.
He designed sex to procreate, to fill the earth
Like seeds contained in the pod.

The marriage bed is undefiled
When two people come together in love.
If sex is just to fulfill our lust
It's an abomination to our Father above.

The ravages caused to our body
Will affect generations to come.
AIDS and Herpes, to name just two
When to wrong desires we succumb.

Only as we ask forgiveness
Will Jesus' blood cover our sin.
Then healing can finally take place
Don't wait – let it begin.

The Lost

Most people are so busy
That they don't think about death.
They have so many things to do
And right now, they have breath.

They seldom seem thankful for that
They just take life for granted.
Their confidence is in themselves
And this is firmly planted.

When there is a little extra time
They need to relax and have fun.
Isn't that what life is all about
After a job well done?

They have no thought for eternity
It never crosses their mind.
The devil, who is prince of this world
Has caused them to be blind.

Until someone, who loves the Lord
Witnesses to them and reveals the truth.
They go on walking in the dark
But many a believer just stands aloof.

Fear of rejection or business
Keeps us from obeying Jesus' command.
Yet, when we respond, and they are saved
There is no feeling so grand.

I AM
SPEAKING

To Unbelievers

WARNING

A Fool

Earth's groanings are getting louder
The end time is drawing near.
Already many are running about
Filled with worry and fear.

Only those who are intimate with Jesus
Will shine like the morning sun.
No matter what is happening around us
We will stand firm – we will not run.

For we are standing on God's Word
The steady rock in any crisis.
Safe and secure in our Father's arms
Whether the cause is nature or Isis.

We know from the Book of Revelation
That things are going to get worse.
Many will blaspheme and curse our God
But we've been delivered from the curse.

We're looking forward to a new Heaven and earth
One where Jesus will reign and rule.
If you haven't made Him Lord of your life
Then we'd have to say – "You are a fool."

WARNING

DEAD MAN WALKING

If your spirit-man is dead
You're not really alive.
Like someone who is drowning
And just trying to survive.

You may go through life smiling
Thinking all is well,
While the truth of the matter
Is a place reserved in Hell.

People have no inkling
You seem successful and secure.
There is an emptiness inside
For which Jesus is the only cure.

Then, there are those in prison
Who have broken the laws of man.
Now, they must pay the price
For letting things get out of hand.

But if they encounter Jesus
And they are born again.
Then they are free indeed
For He's forgiven all their sin.

It's better to be physically behind bars
And have your spirit-man free.
Than to be a dead man walking
Who is blind and cannot see.

That eternity stretches ahead of him
A time of bleakness and pain.
He thought he was such a success in life
But remorse will be his final refrain.

DRUNKENNESS
Proverbs 29:1

Wine is a mocker, beer a brawler
Those led astray by them are not wise.
They promise fun and popularity
But they are just heartache in disguise.

Anything that alters your thinking
Makes you behave in abnormal ways.
You lose all inhibition
Your mind is in a daze.

No one deliberately becomes an alcoholic
They think that they are in control.
In reality they are sliding downward
Satan has destruction as his goal.

It's far safer to avoid temptation
Than to deal with it once it's begun.
Only when you cry out to Our Father
Can this victory ever be won.

FAITH

Faith is the belief that God is real
This fact is oh so true.
If you don't believe that He exists
Satan has blocked your view.

Just look around at the universe
Do you think this all happened by chance?
Man thinks he is so smart
Yet, God knew this in advance.

Just the intricate design of the human body
How God made it to change and grow.
Each tiny cell knows its job
That's more than most men know.

How can we be so ignorant?
When proof stares us in the face.
We should be thankful that God is patient
And doesn't wipe out the whole human race.

We need to awake from our stupor
And realize that God is real.
The evidence surrounds us on every side
We can't depend on what we feel.

Eternity will be a very long time
To realize we made a mistake.
We've based our belief on the wrong thing
And Hell will be our fate.

FUTURE FATE

If the joy of God is not present
The death sentence is still in effect.
Satan has won the battle
And his child, he has come to collect.

Jesus has died to save us
But we still have the right to choose.
Don't harden your heart with sin
And your salvation, eternally lose.

Why settle for a temporal reward
Instead of one that is eternal?
Life on earth is short, at best
But death is always terminal.

God loves each child that he created
He desires that we spend eternity with Him.
He wants to restore and save us
While Satan comes to condemn.

We can only choose while we're alive
Death will be too late.
So, decide now, to follow Jesus
Or hell will be your fate.

Unbeliever Repent

Belief without repentance
Is not belief at all.
If you don't turn in another direction
You are headed for a fall.

Even the demons believe
For they know that God is real.
So just saying that you believe
Is merely expressing something you feel.

If you are not willing to change directions
And turn your life around,
You are simply fooling yourself
And walking on dangerous ground.

For true repentance in your heart
Causes a one-hundred-eighty-degree turn.
Now you are walking with Jesus
And are ready to listen and learn.

I AM
SPEAKING

To Me Personally

LAUNCHING PAD

The Lord's Table is my launching pad
Where I start out my day.
I spend that time with Jesus
Who is the Life and the Way.

He shares His grace and mercy
Which I certainly don't deserve.
But the desire is planted within me
To go out today and serve,

To share the love of Jesus
With everyone I meet.
So many are discouraged
Downtrodden and in defeat.

They need to meet my Jesus
Who will turn their lives around.
Show then what truly living is like
That they are walking on Holy Ground.

With the Holy Spirit within me
I can face and conquer every foe.
Now I am more than a conqueror
And can strike the enemy a fatal blow.

Because I started my day with Jesus
He gives me strength and wisdom for each day
Excitement and challenges lie ahead
So why start out any other way?

HEAVEN BOUND

Hallelujah I've passed over
I'm on the other side.
I've met my Bridegroom face to face
And soon I'll be His Bride.

So, have a great celebration
Dance, and clap, and sing.
If you could see what I see
To this life you'd never cling.

Jesus is more than I ever dreamed
Heaven is such a beautiful place.
When we've loosed this bond of humanity
That's also God's mercy and grace.

Don't be sad that I am gone
Just look forward to joining me here.
Live your life for Jesus
And the way will be made clear.

I'll be waiting for you to join me
After you've fulfilled your destiny.
We'll have another celebration
For indeed, we've been set free.

MY DESIRE

I want to be a sunbeam
When I walk into a room.
Light chases out the darkness
Joy replaces the gloom.

I want to be Jesus with skin on
For the ones who are lost,
To show them the Father's love
That will lead them to the cross.

I want to be a listening ear
To those who are lonely and weak,
Share their burden with them
Show them Jesus is the one they seek,

I want to be a watchman on the wall
So I can see the danger ahead,
To remind them that Jesus won the battle
So, there is nothing to dread.

I want to be a voice in the wilderness
Speaking truth to those I meet,
That they will give their lives to You
Then, our journey together will be sweet.

I want to see with Your eyes
So I recognize those who are blind,
To lead them to the Great Physician
There healing they can find.

I want to love with Your love
Even toward my enemy,
And somehow, they may come to know
That Jesus can set them free.

I just want to be all You want me to be
Then I'll be fruitful in every way.
You've blessed me so I can be a blessing
Now joy will fill my every day.

Praises

Lord, I don't play an instrument
When I sing it's probably off-key.
I want to pour out my praise
And worship unto Thee.

Holy Spirit, pluck the strings of my heart.
Let praise and worship fill the air.
Lord, bend your ears to hear
Let me know You are there.

You see the longings of my heart
Just to sit at Your feet in awe and wonder.
In my inner most being
There is hidden so much hunger.

Just to join the angel chorus
As they praise and magnify Your Name.
I want to soar on wings of praises.
Quiet: I can't remain.

So, I'll praise You in my heart.
You know what is in there.
May it bring You joy
To know how much I care.

My Garden

I can't garden in the dirt anymore
So, I'm working in God's garden now.
I'm sowing seeds like crazy
Sometimes I weed, sometimes I plow.

The Son is always shining here
The rain of the Spirit is the morning dew.
Each day is another surprise
It's always challenging, always new.

The bugs of deceit still have to be watched
But the Master Gardner is always near.
When something is beyond my expertise
I just whisper the problem in His ear.

Then I will know the answer
I just spray His Word all over the place.
Soon the plants are sturdy and strong
No sign of a bug, not even a trace.

As the plants grow and blossom
What a sight they are to those around.
I wouldn't go back to what I had before
For the perfect garden I have found.

Lost

It's hard being ninety-two
In an electronic generation.
I feel like most of the time
My mind is on vacation.

When I'm dealing with some companies
They want my four-digit pin
And my online password,
I just can't seem to win.

It's really kind of funny
When I can't prove that I exist.
I guess when I
just up and die
I won't even be missed.

FERTILIZER

When I die, I take off this old body
Like a coat that was a total mess.
And take from precious Jesus'
His robe of righteousness.

I don't care what they do with the old coat
It would stink unless they bury it deep.
I think it would be such fun
If they just throw me on my compost heap.

This coat will be burned to ashes
That will fertilize a beautiful rose.
This brings beauty into the world
A body in a coffin will just decompose.

My spirit is now in heaven
With no need for that earth suit anymore.
But the rose will stand in remembrance
Of the life I lived before.

A life given completely to Jesus
To glorify and honor His name.
Those who knew me will rejoice and be glad
And someday they will do the same.

My Personal Calling Statement

GOD has made me one of His secretaries
I just listen, then write things down.
A lot of the poems are edifying
Many with His truths abound.

There are those that give us hope
That God is still in control.
Others encourage us to go out
To bring other sheep into His fold.

Some speak of God's love for us
Many praise Him in return.
They tell of His forgiveness
It's free – something we can't earn.

They speak of Heaven and Hell
Some stern warnings to pastors out there.
The glory must all belong to God
And that's what I have to share.

ACKNOWLEDGMENTS

I would dearly like to thank:

The Holy Spirit, who gives these poems to me.

&

Barbara Creighton, who paid to have this book published. She is my partner in crime and the wind beneath my wings when they are drooping.

Lynn Smith & *Jan Galebian* for helping me organize this work.

Alice Neer for so much computer work, she saved my sanity.

Glennis McDonald, my daughter, for listening and all her editing.

Don and Cheryl Bartlett, who bought my computer & printer and help me with technology whenever I'm stranded.

Mike and Debbie Bartlett, who help me financially, so I can listen.

Stacie Jennings for her expert advice.

Coenraad Brand for the photograph.

Zack Mason for preparing this book's interior for publication.

Fran Stewart for all her copyediting and *Matt Smartt* for creating such a beautiful cover.

To *Mike & Jeannie O'Donnell, Pastor Patrick Ballington, Stacie Jennings*, and my sons, *Don & Mike*, for reviewing the contract for me.

And to *all of my friends* who encourage me and keep me accountable!

ABOUT THE AUTHOR

Beverly Bartlett was born in 1927 at Piedmont Hospital in Atlanta, Georgia, the baby of her family with all of her siblings at least 14 years older! She graduated in 1948 from *The University of Georgia* with a degree in Zoology, intending to become a lab technician. Yet, her plans, as she says, "went to the dogs" when she met her future husband, Rayburn, a veterinarian.

God soon blessed them with 3 children: Don, Mike, & Glennis, and 8 grandchildren & great-grandchildren. Unfortunately, for several of their decades together, Rayburn suffered from a serious disability, through which Beverly consistently cared for him. After 52 years of marriage, he went to be with the Lord.

Beverly attended Bible College for several years and says the Lord began giving her poems in the mid-1990s during times of prayer. He continues to do so today.

This is her 3rd book and, even at 93, she enjoys studying God's word and hopes to soon graduate from the School of Discipleship in Gainesville, Georgia.

She currently resides in Cleveland, Georgia surrounded by family and friends.

She is still learning.

INDEX OF POEMS